AF594155

Punto Tagliato Lace

Punto Tagliato Lace

Nenia Lovesey

DRYAD PRESS LTD, LONDON

ACKNOWLEDGMENT

I wish to thank Joan Merrifield, Liz Landry, Vera Nichols, Shirley Warren, Iris Walbank, Nina Devereux and the Liers Ladies who allowed me to use their work to illustrate this book.

Thanks also to Ann Aldridge, Pat Gibson, Cath Barley and May Arnfield for the use of the photographs of old lace; Jani Dubrick for the design of the Hahlah cloth; Ann Pugh who typed the manuscript; and Roy Barley who took the photographs.

Without the help of Nina Devereux and my poor husband Les, who yet again, has stood the test of being the other half of the production line, I don't think this book would ever have reached its final stages.

First published 1986

ISBN 0 8521 9632 6

Typeset by Tek-Art Ltd, Kent
and printed in Great Britain by
Butler and Tanner Ltd
Frome and London
for the publishers
Dryad Press Ltd
8 Cavendish Square
London W1M 0AJ

Contents

Photo 1 A piece of old lace showing the use made of the warp and weft of the material. The diagonal and curved sections of the design have been laid and couched over the top of the remaining threads of the material

1 *How it all began*

Needlelace, as we know it today began in the early sixteenth century, but the techniques that have been the inspiration for this book came much earlier. All forms of cut-work came under the heading of Punto Tagliato, while drawn thread techniques were known as Punto Tirato. In some cases the two types of work were intermingled with surface stitchery. All these forms of needlework gave an openwork effect and over the years the background material became less obvious, until only a framework of threads held all the stitchery together, giving us the needlepoint lace of the type we know now. These lace-like embroideries appear to have originated in southern Europe and slowly to have found their way across the continent to the northern countries of Norway, Sweden and Russia.

For many years the designs relied very much on the warp and weft threads of the material. Then, at a much later date, another method was used that allowed the designs to become less stylized and less formal. This method used a light wooden frame on which threads were fastened, first from one side to the other, then top to bottom, then crossing and interlacing diagonally. Under this maze of threads was fastened, usually with gum, a piece of fine lawn known as *Quintain*, named after the town in Brittany where the best quality material was made.

The network of threads was then sewn to the lawn background using close buttonhole stitch, worked over a fine cord, with very small stitches. The superfluous parts of the material were cut away afterwards, so that the design remained in the background lawn. The buttonholed edge gave a slightly raised effect and was sometimes wrongly called Punto a Reticella.

The cut-work known as Reticella or Greek lace is believed to have originated in the Ionian Isles. As Greece had close connections with the Venetian Republic, it is not hard to imagine the one type of lace changing in character as it travelled along its path.

More complex stitches were introduced and improvements made in the way in which they were worked, thus by the middle of the sixteenth century the linen threads of the foundation material were dispensed with and the Punto in Aria had been invented, leaving the way open for the arrival of the lovely Point de Venise.

In 1558 Matteo Pagan published the *Glory and Honour of Cut Laces and Open Laces*. Let us hope this book can bring back some of the 'Glory' because, when it is worked well, Punto Tagliato can hold its own with other forms of lace. There is no reason why new methods of working and modern designs should not be introduced and this book is being written for now, so although it is based on the original cut-work, it will appeal to the present in the same way as needlepoint and bobbin lace does.

Very briefly the different methods of working some of these cut-works through the ages will be given, although not in their chronological order. We will start with the most simple form and work through to that which inspired this book, then hopefully beyond with our own twentieth-century version.

2 Preparation

Fig. 1 Couching the laid thread – the cordonnet in needlemade lace

A number of the following laces are worked in the hand. When this is the case, care must be taken not to draw stitches tight or the work puckers, but having said this, it is also important to keep a constant tension or the work looks untidy.

If it is necessary to work on a backing material use a twill or glazed cotton. Never a wool or hairy type of cloth because the small hairs in the material can become caught up in the work. It is also advisable to place a piece of draughtsman's linen or acetate film over the pattern to stop the point of the needle penetrating the surface of the paper. When the design is traced directly onto the material being worked and a backing is still called for, it is necessary only to tack round the outside of the design to keep the tension on the material.

In some cases the design has to be couched to the backing material, this is done by using a separate needle and fine thread. The thread is knotted and brought up through the backing material from beneath, over the thread that is being laid, which is called the cordonnet, then the needle is taken back through the base material at right angles to the cordonnet at the same point as it came up or as near as possible. The laid thread stays on the top of the design at all times, at no point is it taken through the base material. At the end of any part of the design where the thread has to be cut, overlap where it began with three or four couch stitches.

For certain types of lace embroideries it is impossible to work satisfactorily in the hand and some form of frame must be used. The advantages of using a frame far outweigh the slight trouble spent on the mounting. A simple roller type frame is adequate. Turn down a small single hem at the top of the material to be mounted. Fold the material in half to find the centre and place a pin in at this point, while finding the centre of the tapes or webbing at the top and bottom of the frame. Pin the centre of the material to the centre of the tapes. Topsew the material from the centre out to the side of the tape in both directions. Repeat this on the opposite roller.

Put in the side laths of the frame and peg or screw out taut. The quickest method of stretching at the sides is by means of tape and pins as shown in Fig. 2.

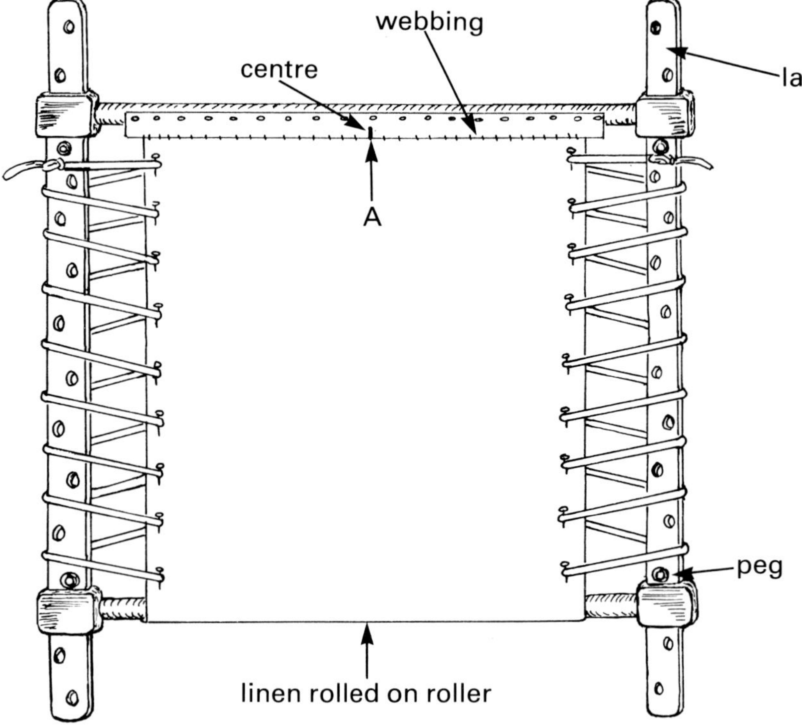

Fig. 2 Slate frame. Turn down ½in (12mm) at the top of the material to be mounted. Find its centre. Pin this to the centre of the webbing (A) of the roller and topsew the two edges securely from the centre outwards. Repeat this on the opposite roller. Put in the side laths and peg out. The method of stretching at the sides is shown. The turned-in edge is laced by means of tape and steel pins

3 Point Coupé

Point Coupé was one of the first 'laces' and was extensively used on the Continent and in England from the fourteenth to the sixteenth centuries, after which it was superseded by Reticella.

'Point' is the French name for a stitch in every description of needlework. 'Coupé' is French for cut-work. Point Coupé differs very little in character from the Roman, Strasbourg and Venetian embroideries.

It is now called Richlieu embroidery after the cardinal who was the Minister to King Louis XIII of France. Cardinal Richlieu encouraged the workers to use finer linen and thread to compete with the new lace from Venice – Punta in Aria. In this way he established an industry in France that was to follow through, under the guidance of Colbert, the Minister to Louis XIV, to the beautiful Alençon and d'Argentan.

In the old cut-work the linen foundation was cut and buttonholed over. The patterns were more solid and almost completely covered with surface embroidery requiring much patience and time.

The modern Richlieu differs from the old cut-work in as much as the patterns are more open. This is because bars are used to connect one part of the design to the other. Picots are placed centrally on each bar and along the outside edge of the design in some cases. A firm light-weight linen, cambric cotton or silk can be used for this work.

Trace the outline of the pattern onto the material and indicate the lines of the bars. Back the material with either brown paper or draughtsman's linen, to keep the embroidery from puckering while being worked. Run in all the outlines with a double row of running stitches and place a third row one 1/16in (1.5mm) above the other two (Fig. 3.)

All the bars are worked during the process of running in the outline. To make the bar, place three threads across the space that is to be connected, catch the thread well within the edges of the pattern, then buttonhole over all threads. The stitches should be tightly packed and a Bullion picot placed in the centre of each bar. Then carefully buttonhole over the entire outline working over the end stitches of the bars (Fig 4).

Fig. 3 Outlining the design with backstitch

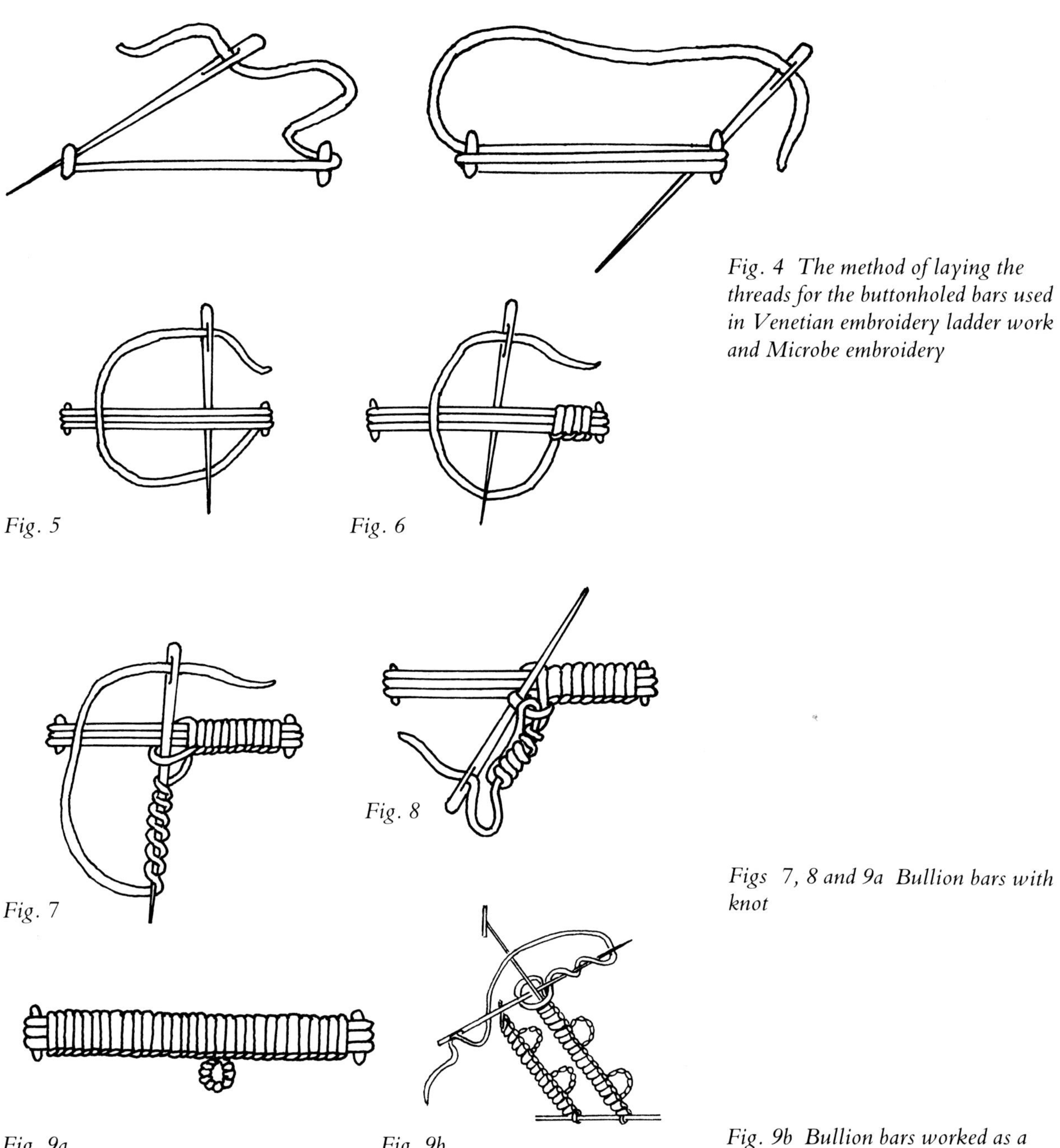

Fig. 4 *The method of laying the threads for the buttonholed bars used in Venetian embroidery ladder work and Microbe embroidery*

Fig. 5

Fig. 6

Fig. 7

Fig. 8

Figs 7, 8 and 9a Bullion bars with knot

Fig. 9a

Fig. 9b

Fig. 9b Bullion bars worked as a filling

Always place the edge of the buttonhole stitches to the edge that is to be cut away. Great care must be taken to keep the stitches even and at the same length. This is the reason for the inside row of running stitches along the outline. If the needle is always inserted just beyond these stitches the width of each line will remain the same. The density of the edge of the work will depend on the closeness of the stitches and size of the thread being used.

If a scalloped outside edge is being worked it can be ornamented with Bullion picots (Figs 7-9). These can be varied in size as they round the scallop by having more, or less, twists round the needle. Next, any surface stitchery is worked, which by tradition consists of any of the following: Seeding, French Knots, Padded Dots, Fly, Stem and Satin stitches.

The cutting away of the fabric from around the design and from under the bars is the last operation. Remove the embroidery from the backing brown paper or draughtsman's linen. If the work has become dirty, squeeze gently in a solution of warm water and Stergene and press while still damp, first on the right side then turn over and press on the wrong side to lift the embroidery stitches. Then carefully cut away the material. A final press will be needed as the work always looks crumpled after the cutting.

Photo 2 Embroidery in the process of being worked over a machine outline

Fig. 10 This design can be mirror-imaged along the top edge, or it can be laid end to end as a straight length, or curved

Photo 3 Outline and raising worked on the Elna Tx sewing machine. The Elna has been used to set appliqué ready for finishing with hand embroidery and for eyelets and satin stitch on the doll's underwear. *See photograph on page 47*

Photo 4 The same design being worked in the traditional manner by Liz Landry, using silk thread on silk slub material. The photograph shows different stages of the work

4 Bars and picots

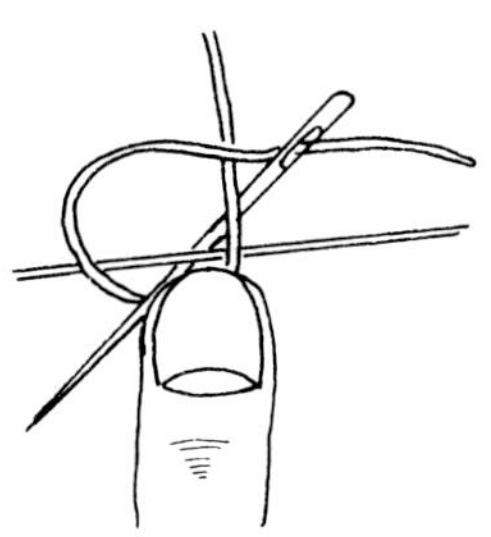

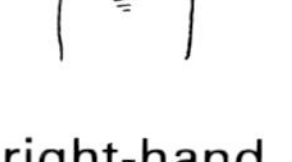

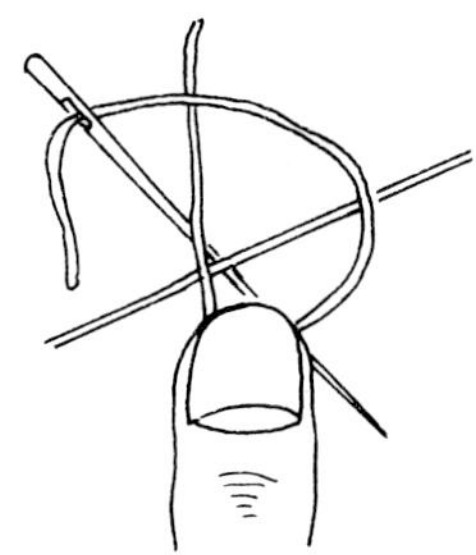

Fig. 11 Knot stitch

KNOT STITCH

Run the working thread in to the point at which the row is to start. Lay the working thread under the thumb and make buttonhole stitch over one thread of the material. This would be identical to working over a cordonnet or couched thread (Fig. 11).

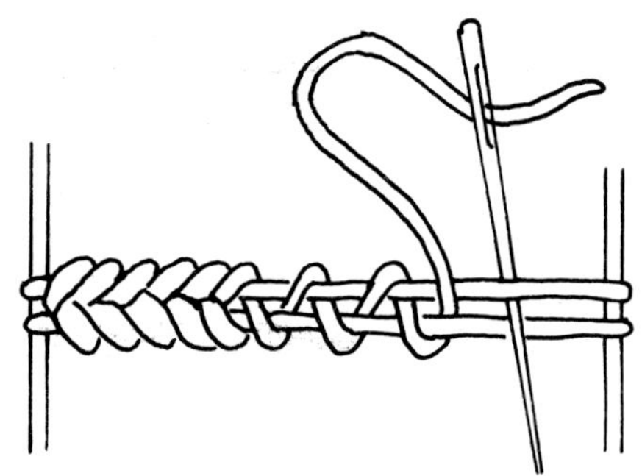

Fig. 12 A woven bar worked over two laid threads

BARS AND PICOTS

Bars

These are used to strengthen cut-work and can either be left plain or ornamented with picots. The most simple of all bars is made over three laid threads, which are then buttonholed over. See Fig. 4 page 12, the use of buttonhole stitches makes it slightly heavier.

WOVEN BAR

This is made over three laid threads, place the threads in the same way as before then work over under and over in one direction and under over the centre thread and under the last thread going in the opposite direction. If using four laid threads, it is under and over two threads all the time. Fig. 12 shows a bar worked over two laid threads.

Do not attempt to work picots on woven bars as the picot will stop the threads from lying close together. It is the woven bar worked over three threads that causes confusion in a number of needlemade laces as its appearance is that of a bobbin lace *bride*.

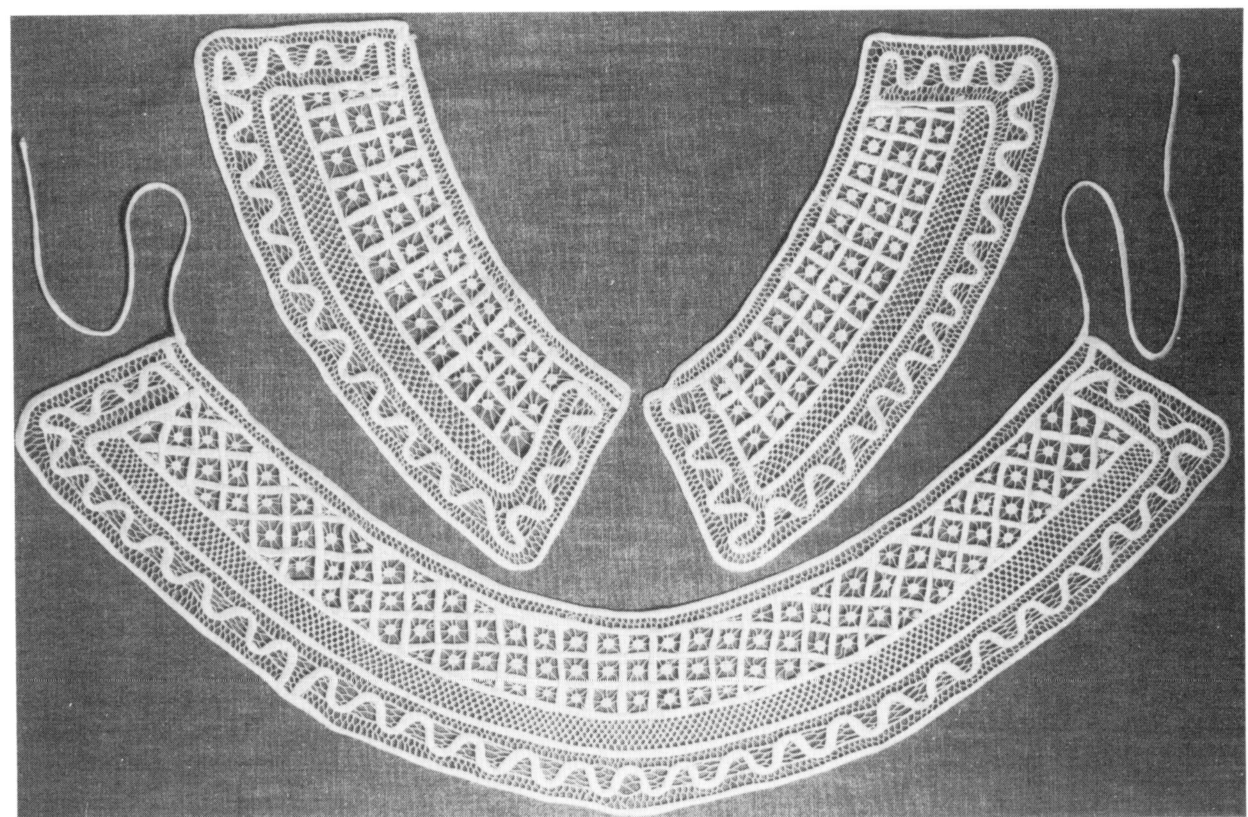

Photo 5 Late nineteenth-century collar and cuffs. Ribbon has been used as a cordonnet and all the stitches have been worked from the edge of the ribbon

Photo 6 A collar based on the previous idea using a fine linen lawn as the base material. The only stitches used are buttonhole, twisted bars and woven rings

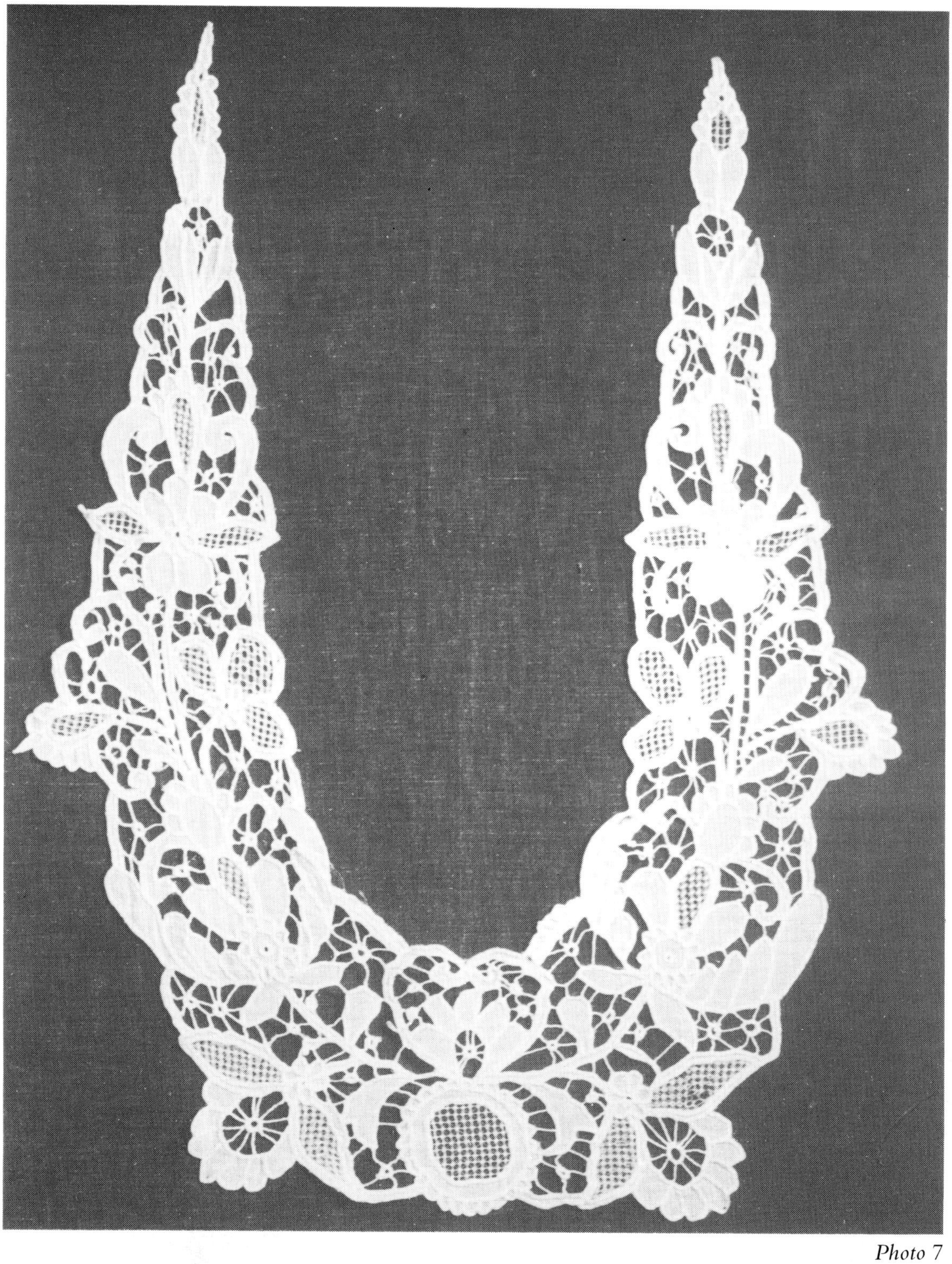

Photo 7

TWISTED BARS

These are made from one point to another, whipping half-way down the laid thread. The needle is then taken through the material at the bottom at a point that will be centre of the next point along the top line.

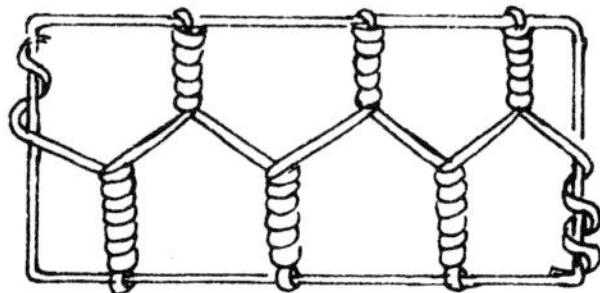

Fig. 13 Twisted bars

CROSSED BARS WITH WHEELS

Take the thread from *A* to *B*, back to *A*, then to *B*. Buttonhole or whip back half-way along the laid threads. Then take the thread to *C*, down to *D*, back to *C* and down to *D*. Buttonhole back to half-way. Take the thread up to *C* and buttonhole back to centre.

★ Whip under *B* over *D* under *A* and take the needle through the last buttonhole stitch on *C* ★.

★★ Whip over *B* under *D* over *A* under *C* ★★ and back to *A*. Buttonhole up to the start of *A*.

The wheel can be made larger by working from ★ to ★, then from ★★ to ★★ taking the needle through the centre buttonhole stitch at *B* then over *D* and continue in this way taking the thread through the next bar back on the way round each time. Remember that *A* always has to be buttonholed back to the start.

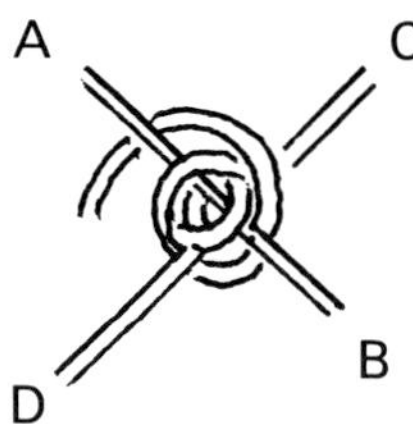

Fig. 14 Working crossed bars with wheels

ALENCON BARS

In needlepoint these are used either as a filling or as a row of light bars. Take the needle up and under two threads of the material, then twist the loop formed over the needle twice before pulling the needle through to form the stitch. Then take the needle through two threads at the base of the row to form a bar. This can be continued along a row (see tablecloth), or can be worked as shown in Fig. 14 as a filling.

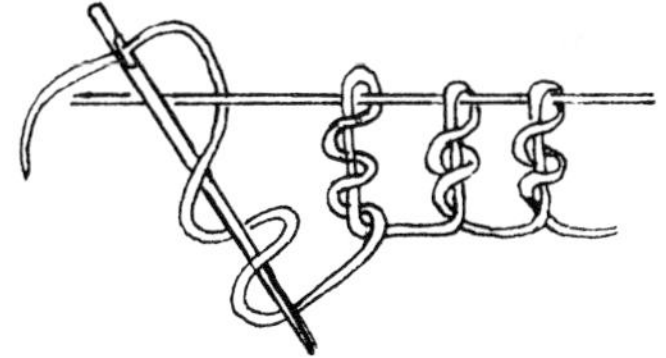

Fig. 15 Alençon bars

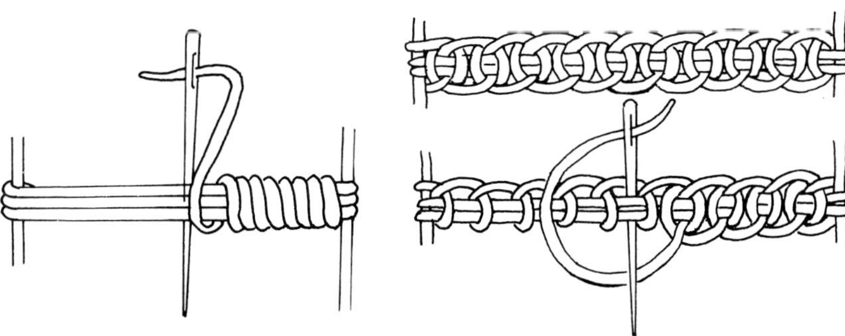

Fig. 16 A whipped bar

Fig. 17 An easy version of the Ardenza bar. The instruction for this can be found in The Technique of Needlepoint Lace

It is advisable to work a square for all the following stitches before trying to fill a shaped space. Having mastered the formation of the patterns it is easier to see how to add or lose stitches when working to a curve. Outline any shaped space with small running stitches to give guidance as to how far the threads should be withdrawn. The running stitches can be removed or covered by a cordonnette once the fillings have been worked. Another useful idea is a cut-out stencil of the shape, which can be laid over the worked sample giving the exact start and end of each row.

Photo 8 Using the same techniques as the previous collar with larger motifs filled with raised dots

Alençon beads

These can also be utilised in combined techniques such as in the tablecloth and the Venetian embroidery, where they are combined with quilting.

Work two rows of buttonhole stitches along opposite sides of a space. The working thread is passed over and down through the top loop, then the needle enters the bottom loop from behind; now make three more loops in the same way into the same space.

The threads of the stitches must lie beside each other.

After the fourth loop, twist the working thread round the bottom buttonhole stitch and carry it through to the next stitch.

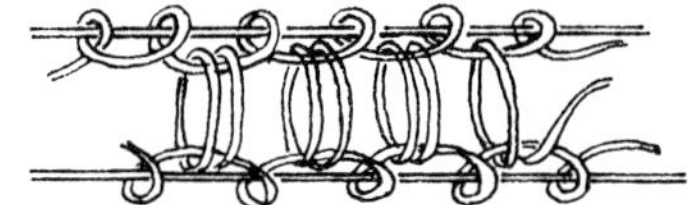

Fig. 18 Alençon beads

BRANCHING BARS

These are made of three bars joined together, connecting three points of an embroidery at one time.

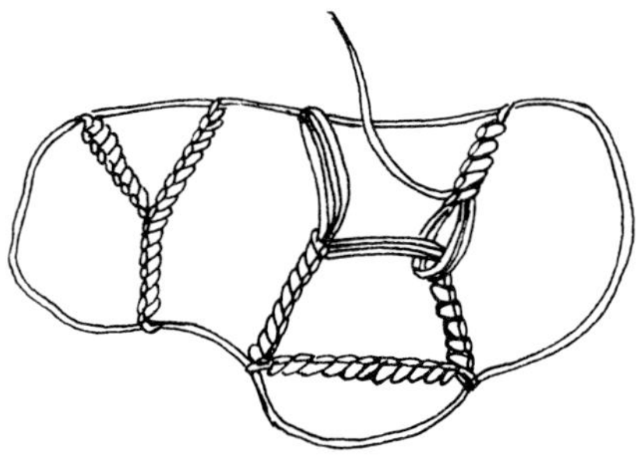

Fig. 19 Branching bars

BULLION BARS (*see Figs 7, 8 and 9*)

Work from left to right along the bar to the position of the first picot. Place the needle back into the down bar of the last buttonhole stitch. Twist the thread six times round the point of the needle.

The thumb is now placed over the twists while the needle is pulled through.

Tighten up the thread to draw the twists into a curve.

This is kept in place by working the next buttonhole stitch against the previous one.

All these bars can be found in different types of cut-work and the drawings clearly show how they are worked.

Picots

PURL

This is the most common in all cut-work.

One row of buttonhole stitches can be worked along the edge of the design before working the purl or it can be worked over the edge of the material. To work the purl, make a buttonhole stitch leaving a loop the length needed for the purl, throw the working thread to the right then down and round to the left. Place the needle behind the buttonhole stitch and through the loop formed by the working thread; pull tight to form a knot.

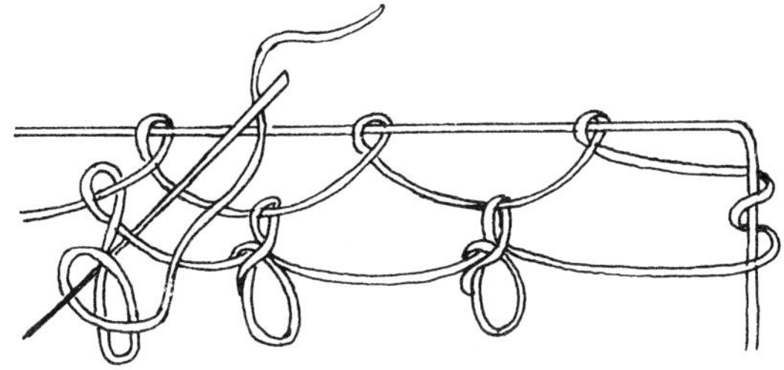

Fig. 20 Purls

LOOP PICOT

The loop picot is worked from right to left if you are right-handed, reverse the movements if left-handed and start from the left.

Work along to the position of the first picot and insert the pin as for Venetian picot. Pass the working thread from right to left under the pin, then still working to the left, over the top of and down behind the bar or foundation threads.

Throw the working thread over the pin to the right.

Make a buttonhole stitch round the picot by taking the working thread under both sides of the loop but over the pin, under the working thread where it emerges from behind the bar, then over the working thread where it is forming the large loop.

Pull tight to form the picot. The spacing of these picots will depend entirely on how and where the picots are being used. Even the length of picots can be varied to form scallops.

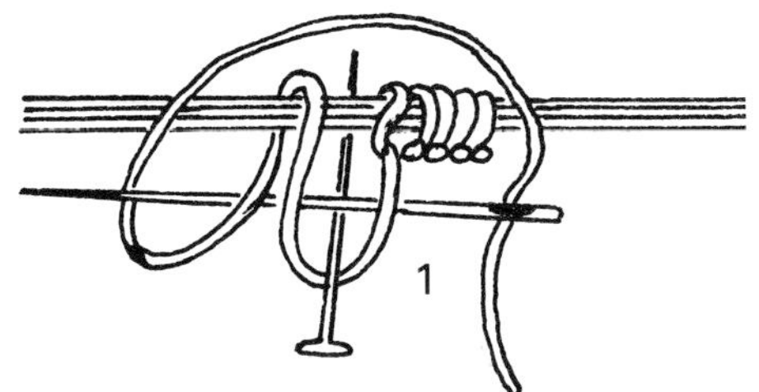

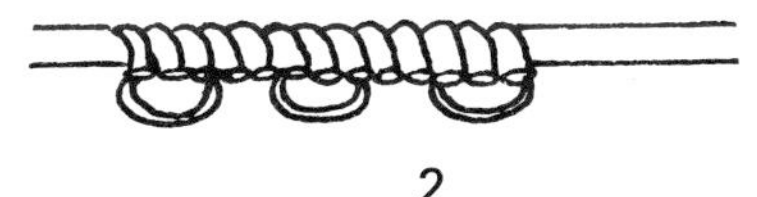

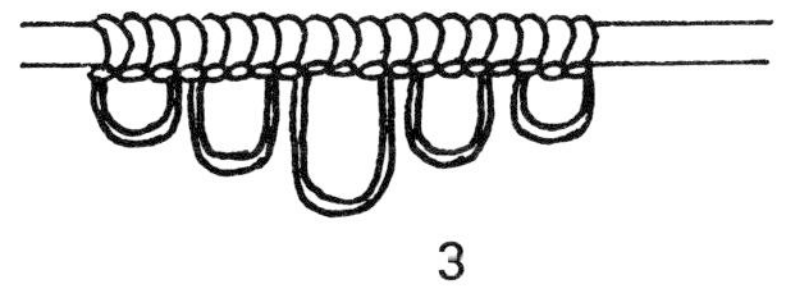

Fig. 21 Loop picot

VENETIAN PICOT

Work the buttonhole bar from right to left. Where the picot is to be worked place a pin into the edge of the material. The needle is taken round the pin to the length required for the picot. Make a buttonhole stitch over the bar, taking the thread under the pin a second time from right to left.

Throw the thread in a loop over the top of the bar and to the right-hand side of the picot.

The thread is then taken over the right-hand side of the first loop, under the working thread, over the pin, under the left-hand side of the loop and over the working thread.

Pull the thread tight forming the end of the picot, buttonhole up the remainder of the loop to the bar.

Continue to buttonhole the foundation threads to position of next picot.

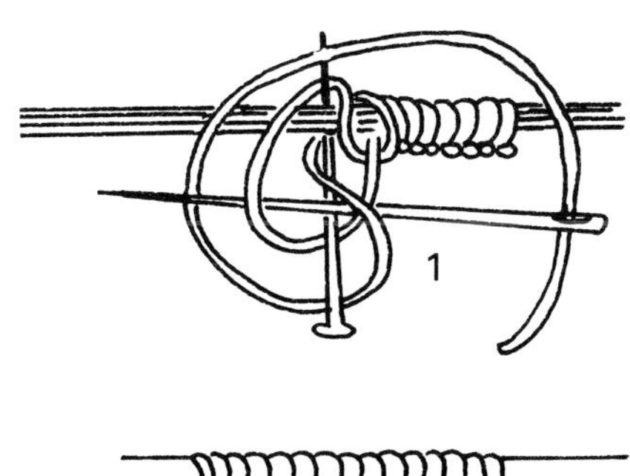

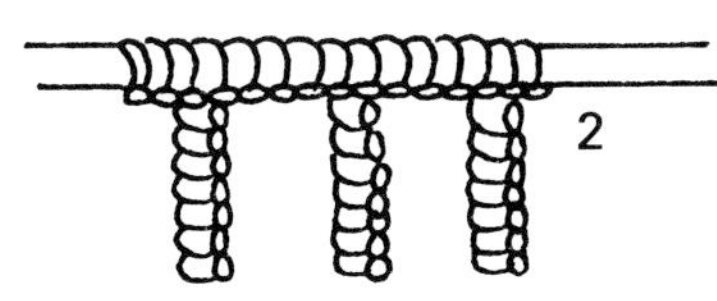

Fig. 22 Venetian picot

5 Broderie anglaise

This is one of the most simple of all open-work embroideries, especially as it is possible to use a sewing machine to make the round eyelets. The Elna Tx does the job with no fuss at all, see Photo 3.

For those of you who prefer to work in the original way, here are some pointers. It is worked in the hand and to look at all worthwhile this is one form of embroidery that has to be carefully executed. Traditionally very few stitches were used, it is the eyelets that distinguish the work. Herringbone, satin, stem, overcasting and buttonhole are the excepted stitches. In some pieces of embroidery the eyelets run down in size until they are too small to be worked in either overcasting or buttonhole stitches, so the last few dots have been worked in French Knots. This is not the usual procedure as raised satin stitch is used in most cases.

The material needs to be even in texture and also be one that will not fray easily. Linen or cotton lawn and cambric give the most satisfactory results.

Check the material for shrinkage before starting any work, by measuring first, then washing and ironing a sample piece. Then measure again and check the two measurements. Personally I always wash and iron any materials to be used as a precaution against shrinkage.

Leave a good margin of material around the outside edge of the design, so that the working of the scalloped edge, which is very much part of broderie anglaise, is easy to handle.

Outline the design with very small running stitches. Never knot the thread, when a new thread is to be run in, overlap the last few stitches. In the same way overlap the first and last stitches of each part of the design. Use mercerised threads corresponding in thickness to the thread of the material. Stranded embroidery cotton is ideal because it can be broken down into any number from one to six strands according to the weight of the material. For padding the shadow eyelets, the satin stitches and the scalloping, a thicker thread than the actual working thread is advisable. A smooth round thread, that will not fluff up or twist, is needed for both eyelet and ladder work. If using stranded cotton, the crewel needles are easiest to thread. Sharps or Betweens size ten can be used for single threads. Embroidery à Broder Sticknadein needles size ten are easy to use when working with Mettler mercerised embroidery/lace cotton 60/2s on fine cambric or lawn.

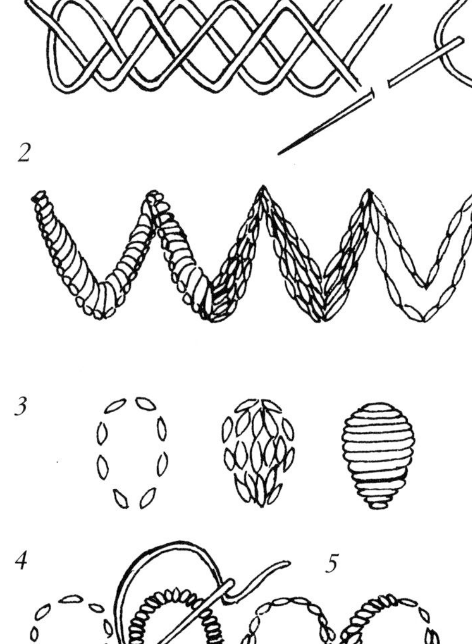

Fig. 23 1. Close herringbone stitch used for the padding under the petals and leaves
2. The back stitch trace, padding and final buttonhole stitch used to work the scallops
3. The three stages of working the padded dots
4. Overcast eyelets
5. Shaded eyelets

A sharp pair of embroidery scissors that cut to the very tips of the blades are needed to make clean incisions in the material and for removing the edge of the material away from the scallops. Other important pieces of equipment needed are different size stilettos. When these are not available, then different size knitting needles can be used. Use a large darning needle, or the type of needle used for sewing up knitting, to pierce the material first; this parts the threads enough to follow through with the stiletto. The threads of the material are likely to snag if a large stiletto is forced through without starting off with a small hole.

Eyelets come in many different sizes and shapes, small round eyelets are pierced with a stiletto then closely oversewn or buttonholed round. The larger holes have an incision made, with sharp scissors, in the form of a cross, the cut threads are folded back then oversewn as above, the raw edges at the back are trimmed away.

Take care not to draw stitches too tight nor overlap the buttonhole or the overcast, just allow each one to be close to its neighbour. The knot of the buttonhole stitches is always placed along the edge that is to be cut.

Shadow eyelets have a padding laid evenly round the circle first, then one half of the circle is made wider with the aid of more rows of stitches. When this is oversewn or buttonholed it forms an assymetric effect. All the padding stitches must be laid within the outline of the shape. To fasten off, run the needle through a few stitches on the wrong side of the work. Remember to thread the needle before cutting off the thread from the reel, there is less likelihood of the thread twisting back on itself and forming a knot. If this does happen, put the point of the needle into the loop of the knot and pull first the thread nearest the material, if this does not release it, pull the thread on the other side of the knot. A quick pull on both sides of the knot will remove the last obstinate little twist. Any persistent twisting of the thread can be helped by taking the needle along the thread to the material, then run the thread between the thumb and first finger from the needle down to the end of the thread. Then bring the needle back up the thread to its original position.

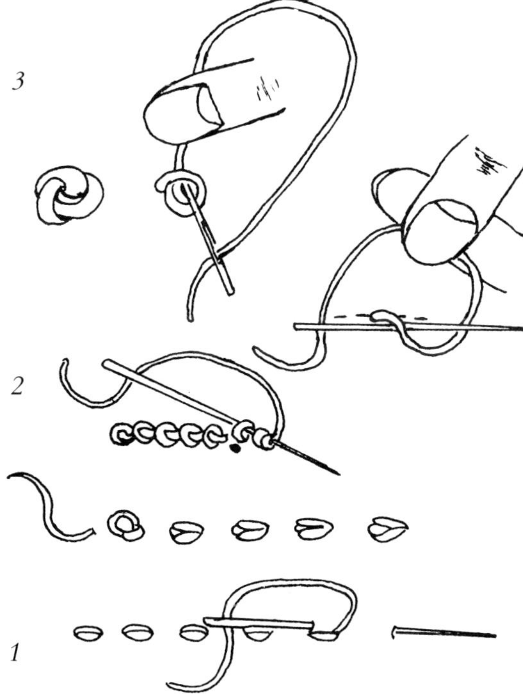

Fig. 24 1. Seeding. Two back stitches laid side by side
2. Knotted stitch consists of one chain stitch, with a back stitch placed in the centre of the chain
3. Bullion rose is worked by placing the thread round the point of the needle, drawing the thread up but not tight. Then taking the needle over the loop just made and down through the centre of the loop

Ladder work or Pisa stitch is the name given to the technique used for scrolls and open-work leaves. First outline with running stitches then work two or three rows for padding. The longest side of the scroll or leaf is worked first, take the stitches round the top and down the other side to the point of the first bar. Work a bar using any of the instructions on pages 16-20, then continue down to the position of the next bar and repeat. The bars must be evenly spaced and lie at the right angle to the curve. Ladder work, as the name suggests, can be worked in straight lines using the same procedure as before, the *rungs* are placed at right angles to the two parallel lines, and the same number of stitches are worked between each rung. The knot of the buttonhole stitch lies to the centre of the ladder and the material is cut away from behind the *rungs*. The sample in Photo 9 plainly shows the lie of the stitches. This technique was used many years ago to join unsightly seams or to add an extra piece of material to lengthen a child's sleeve or hem of a shirt. It was also used to form a *beading* through which ribbon was threaded.

Fig.25

The size of the thread, width of ladder and the distance between the *rungs* should be decided according to the material chosen and the purpose for which it is to be used.

The initial *N* is an example of how ladder work can be used for letters, a very quick way to make a handkerchief into a personal gift. A piece of information perhaps long forgotten is that Pisa work was sometimes called *Grub* work or *Microbe* embroidery, when different shaped curves were used to form the shape of an insect as shown on page 25.

Photo 9 The background of the letter R *is painted with Deka paints in shades of pink and bronze metallic and behind the cut-work is a bronze woven cloth as used in ecclesiastical work. The vague shape follows the outline of the butterfly shown on the opposite page. This piece was worked by Shirley Warren*

Scalloping has a row of running stitches along both top and bottom line, keeping exactly to the edge of the design. The area between the two rows of running stitches is padded with either herringbone or stem stitch. When working the buttonhole, keep all stitches running straight from the top to the bottom line, firmly packed to avoid the material showing through. The scalloping is always the last part of the design to be worked and is not cut away until everything is completed.

Leaves and scrolls are worked in padded satin stitch, first outline with running stitches then fill in with tailors' tacks worked very small. These are worked by taking only a short stitch on the wrong side of the material and longer stitches on the right side. Stagger the rows to avoid troughs appearing when the satin stitch is worked.

Photo 10 Grub work or Pisa work giving a design for a butterfly. The initial N given as a design can be compared with the initial R worked to show how easily the scrolls can be formed to make any letter. This piece was worked by Shirley Warren as part of a box lid

Fig. 26

◁ *Photo 11 A Victorian collar worked in broderie anglaise*

Fig. 27 The designs used for the front edge and the back of the bonnet

Fig. 28 The filling used for the flowers on the dress

Photo 12 A design worked on silk using Gütermann silk thread 100/s

Fig. 29 This design, used on the front of the dress, can be enlarged or reduced, but worked to the given size Gütermann silk, size 100/3s was used for the embroidery and six strands of embroidery cotton were used to work the herringbone stitches for the padding. A transfer of a small spray taken out of context was used for the back of the bonnet

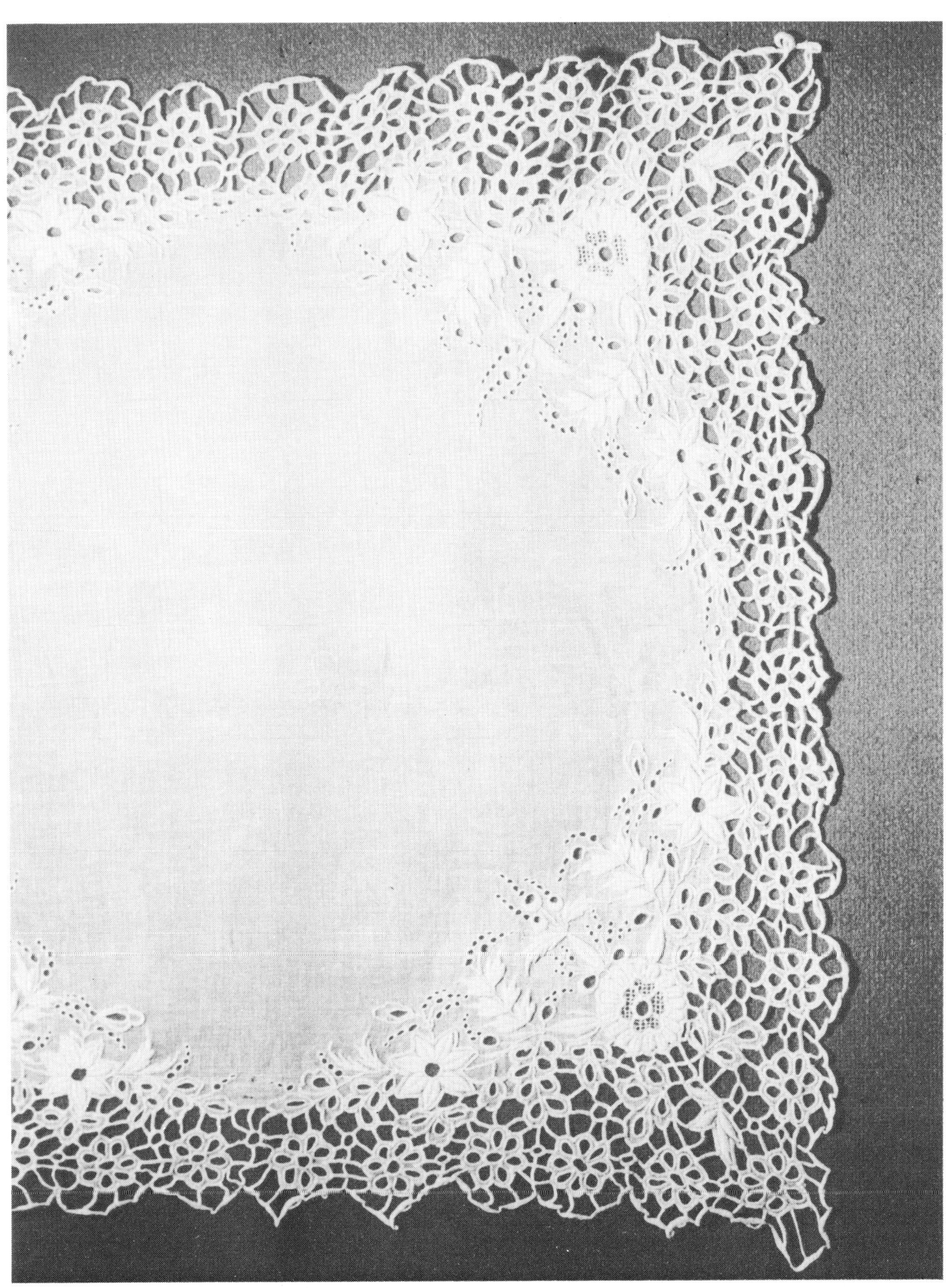

Photo 13 A handkerchief which belongs to Pat Gibson. It is worked on linen lawn. The flowers have lace centres, all petals and leaves are padded and the eyelets are of different size rings, some being padded asymmetric ones. This piece of work shows the progression from bars and buttonholes through to a more solid effect formed by taking the raised work down into the design formed by the bars

6 Coggeshall lace

Tambour work was introduced to Coggeshall (a small town in Essex England) in 1812, when an emigré M. Drago, along with his two daughters, arrived in the town. He opened a tambour room in an old mill and began teaching young local girls the craft of tambouring, which became known locally as Coggeshall lace. There is a little book entitled *Coggeshall Lace* which has been well documented by Mrs Jean Dudding, who with the help of her friends has firmly established this lace once again in the area around Coggeshall. Now Joan Merrifield teaches tambour work at the English Lace School at Rockbere, near Honiton, Devon. Joan's work has been shown on televison both nationally and abroad.

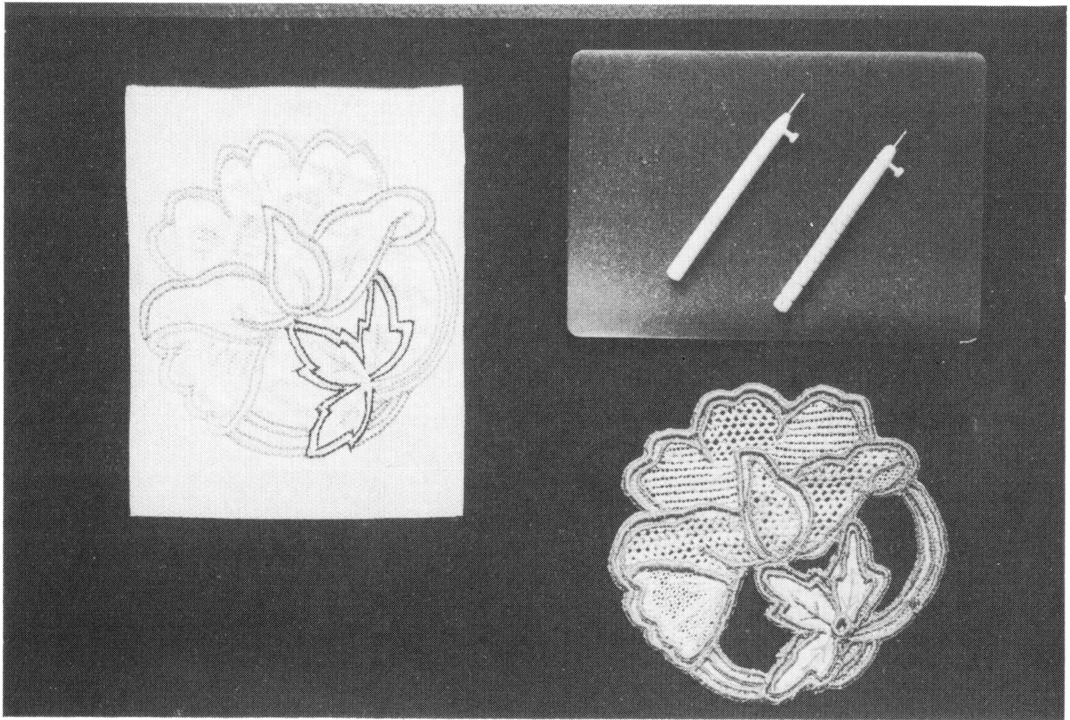

Photo 14 1. The net and muslin which is laid over the design can be pencilled in with a soluble pencil.
2. Two tambour hooks. One has the hook reversed back into the handle while not in use. The other shows the position of the hook in relation to the screw which acts as a guide.
3. This piece of work is finished and has had either the net or muslin cut away leaving the different textures showing. It was worked by Joan Merrifield

7 Tambour work

Tambouring is done with a hook although the finished stitch is identical to that of the chain stitch, which is worked with a sewing needle and thread. It is a more rapid method of producing the same stitch once the technique has been mastered. Tambour work was introduced from the East into Europe around 1760 and traditionally it was worked on material. The material was held taut in a special frame that looked a little like a drum, this was held between the knees which left both hands free to manipulate the thread.

It was not the technique that was new when introduced to Coggeshall, only the fact that it was worked on net rather than on material.

The small round embroidery frames pull the mesh of the net out of shape so it is best to use a slate frame. Mount the frame with cotton sheeting, pin the net to this, then cut the sheeting away from behind the net, it is essential that the net is held taut in the frame. The net that is available today has a different mesh to the old cotton net and the shape of the holes changes the character of the design. Study the net you are using and you will find that the holes in one direction are further apart than the holes in another direction.

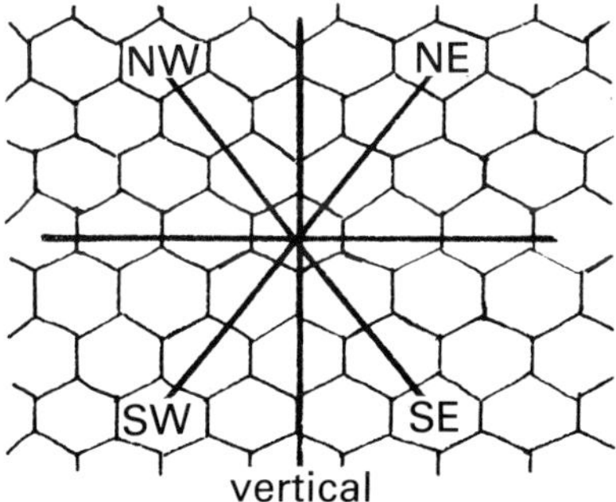

Fig. 30 The directions of the holes in the net when it is pinned correctly to the backing material in the frame

When applying the net to the sheeting the horizontal holes should be lying close to each other as should the holes lying in a line running north-west to south-east and from north-east to south-west. This fact decides the direction of the filling stitches.

Find a tin or container with a lid which is large enough to hold the ball of thread comfortably. Pierce a hole in the lid to let the thread run through. The pierced hole must be smoothed off otherwise the thread will snag. With the ball of thread in the container and the start of the thread through the hole in the lid, place the lid on tight and stand the container under the frame.

The thread to start with is D.M.C. mercerised cotton No. 80 or Fils à Dentelles No. 70. While a finer thread such as Retors d'Alsace No. 60 is used for the filling stitches.

There are two sizes of net suitable for tambouring, cotton net No. 844 for learning to use the hook and for practising the stitches, and cotton net No. 969 for working the lace.

The design can be transferred using a water soluble pencil and tracing off the design while it is held directly under the net. Originally the design was tacked to one side of the net and offered up periodically against the net while the worker mentally followed through until having to offer up the design again. Experienced workers who worked on repeat designs could translate the design by counting or even 'eyeing' the holes of the net. Once the tambour hook is mastered, a very good exercise is to do a 'free-hand drawing' using the hook as a pencil. The tambour hook resembles a crochet hook, except that the hook of the tambour is recessed into the shaft instead of protruding at the end as it does with a crochet hook. The hook of the tambour is recessed to allow it to be withdrawn back through the mesh of the net without catching up the threads. Hold the hook in the hand, in the same way as you would hold a pen ready to write, on top of the net.

The other hand manipulates the thread under the frame, using the thumb and first finger to hold the thread. There is a marker, or a screw, that shows the position of the actual hook. This is used as a guide to make sure the hook and screw are facing in the same direction. The two hands work in conjunction with each other and must be kept very relaxed while working as this will affect the tension of the work. When starting, the hook and the marker/screw should always face the direction in which the work is to proceed. To join the thread to the net, place the hook through a hole in the mesh, the hand holding the thread under the frame places the thread into the hook. Bring the hook with the thread, held taut around it, up through the mesh to form a loop, keep this loop on the hook.

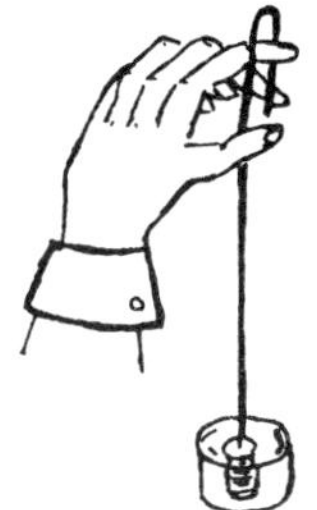

Underneath the frame there will be two threads, one attached to the ball of thread, the other the start of the thread, both being held between your finger and thumb. Take the hook down through the next mesh and pick up the short thread. To do this, the hook will have to be twisted 180 degrees between your finger and thumb of the hand holding the hook, this allows the hook to clear the net to bring the thread up. Take the second loop through the first making a tambour stitch. Turn the hook back to its original position, with the marker/screw facing away from you, and insert it back into the first hole of the mesh where you started and again pick up and make a loop from the short thread. The hook must be turned round the 180 degrees every time it comes back up through the net, this is very important.

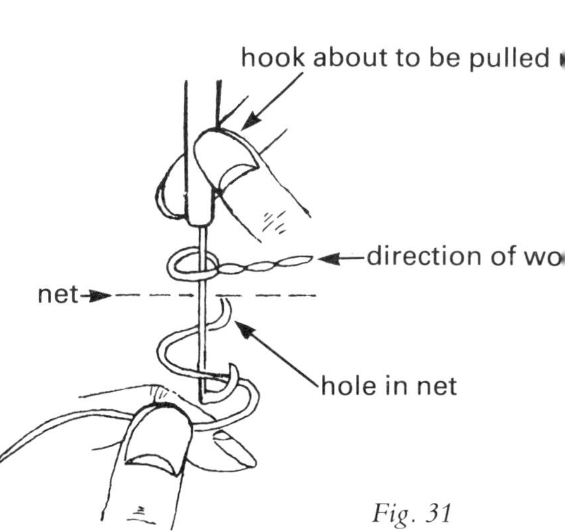

Fig. 31

Now bring the short end of the thread right through to the top of the net, this secures the thread. Insert the hook into the net behind the fastening on and pick up the long thread from under the frame. You are now ready to start tambouring.

Work very slowly until the rhythm of the formation of the stitch has been acquired.

1. Keep the hook and marker/screw facing the direction of progress and insert the hook down through the next hole in the net.
2. Wind the thread around the hook one and a half times with the hand under the frame and keep the thread held in the direction of progress.
3. Twist the handle round between first finger and thumb through 180 degrees.
4. With the handle upright, press the smooth side of the hook onto the front of the hole in the net to stop the hook snagging the net as it comes back up through the net.
5. Pull the hook with looped thread through the net to the top surface.
6. Turn the handle back to its original position.
7. Insert the hook into the next hole, wind the thread round the hook, follow instructions 3 and 4. Pull the loop through the net and right through the loop on the hook.

You are now ready to work the next chain. In movements 2 and 3, the winding and the twisting should be in the same direction, clockwise or anticlockwise.

Always return the twist (6) in reverse direction to (3). These are the basic movements of the stitch which should be practised in all directions, horizontally, diagonally and vertically, both backwards and forwards (figs. 30 and 31).

In Coggeshall lace a chain stitch is frequently worked from side to side over a line of tambouring. This is called the Zig-zag stitch and once this is worked it is safe to cut away the net up to this strengthened line of tambouring. This has been used on the tablecloth where ever the net and muslin have been cut away.

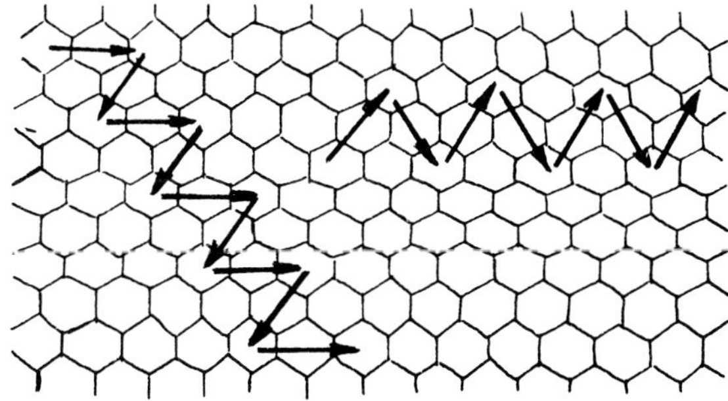

Fig. 32 Zig-zag stitch

Finishing off is done in the same way by working one or two knot stitches. Cutting off a thread must be done with care. Hold the thread tightly in the hand under the frame and hold the last loop on the hook tight above the frame. Give a quick jerk with the hook and the thread round the hook will snap (hopefully). It is a case of 'if at first you don't succeed, try and try again'. Once the thread is broken, insert the hook into the net from below and pull the short end back down through the net. If in doubt, pull the loop right through the last chain, as when finishing off crochet, cut the thread and weave the end into the back of the work with a needle.

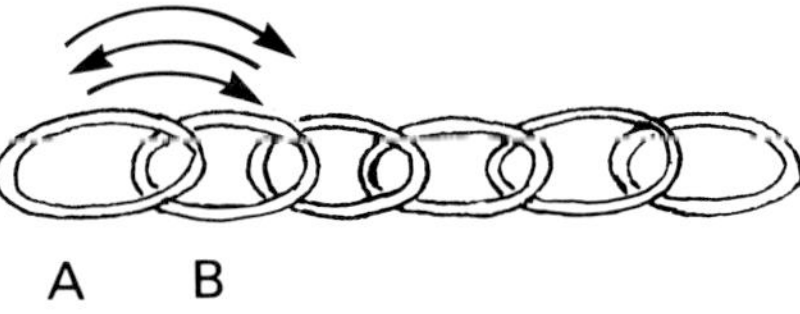

Fig. 33 Beginning or finishing off by making one or two knot stitches in following way:
Work three small chains
1. From A to B
2. From B to A
3. From A to B

There has purposefully been no mention of left or right

hands, either can be used above or below the net and each reader will find a method of using the hook that suits her. It will also be found that it is perhaps easier going in one direction than another.

Just one other point, corners and points become rounded when tambouring due to the mesh of the net. In order to rectify this always proceed into a hole beyond the point or corner and back into the corner chain of the design, then work on along the line of the design.

DRAW-BACK STITCH

1. Insert the hook at *A* and pull the loop through the hole.
2. Insert the hook into hole *B* and pull the loop through the hole and through the loop on the hook.
3. Loosen the thread at the back and gently draw the loop back.
The hook is then inserted into hole *A* again. Pull the loop through the hole and through the loop on the hook.
4. Insert the hook into the hole at *C* and make a tambour chain stitch.

Repeat from steps 2 to 4 up to *D* and back to *C* and chain to *E*.

Repeat steps 2 to 4 and on to the next hole on the bottom line.

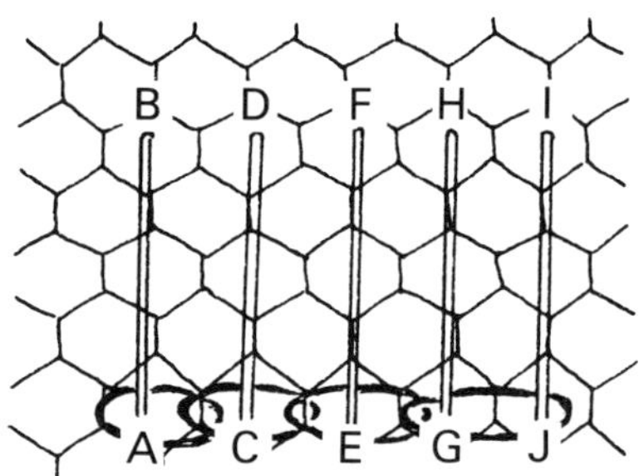

Fig. 34 Draw back

NEAT STITCH

This is worked in the same way as Zig-zag but at a sharper angle without the row of tambour stitches under it. It can be used as a filling stitch or to strengthen the outside edge of lace.

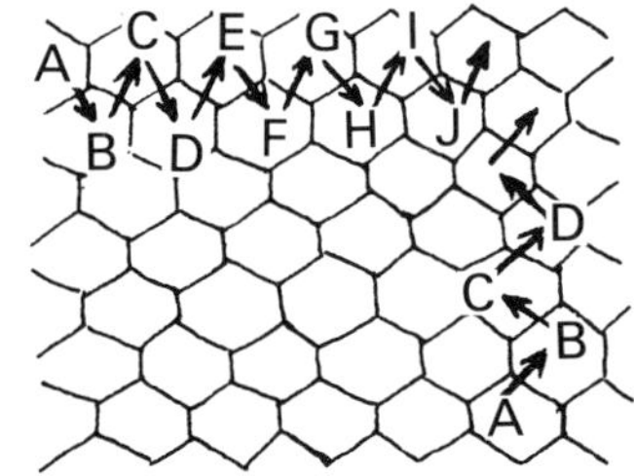

Fig. 35 Neat stitch

HONEYCOMB STITCH (large)

Each complete honeycomb hole is worked in two rows.

Fasten on the thread then work in this sequence, *A B C A D C E D F E G E*, make the return journey by going back to G, then to *E H I E C I J C B J K B*.
An enclosed section of a design formed by two repeats of pattern is called a *casket*. In tambour work these caskets are often filled with needlemade stitches. The following stitches can be worked between rows of Neat stitch or Zig-zag.

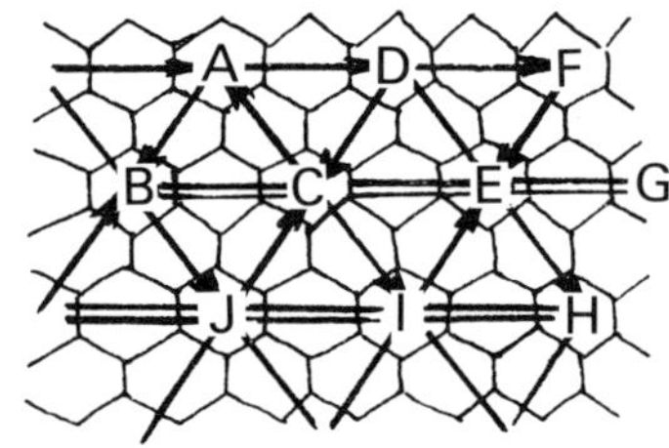

Fig. 36 Honeycomb stitch

Filling stitches can be used on any area of the net that is contained within the tamboured design.

BUTTONHOLE FILLING

This can be used as a surface stitch for Venetian embroidery or as a filling for any net when working with a tambour hook. The diagram shows it worked in graduated points up and down the single mesh. Depending on the weight of material being used it can be worked over two, three or four threads. The finer the threads the smaller the design appears and if working with muslin or linen lawn it is possible to work the stitch without counting threads.

A soluble embroidery pencil can be used to mark the progress of the stitch. With net, one mesh only holds the stitch, the rest lies on the surface of the net. The same must apply when working on material, take up just enough of the threads to hold the shape of the stitch, the rest of the stitch lies on the surface.

Using the same principle as above the filling can look completely different if the first row is worked in graduated points, then for the second row turn the work upside down. Start the row six meshes down and work three stitches up to meet the bottom stitch of the first row.

Take the needle through the two loops of that stitch, then work three stitches down to form the point of connection for the third row which is worked in the same way as the first, always turning the work at the start of each row.

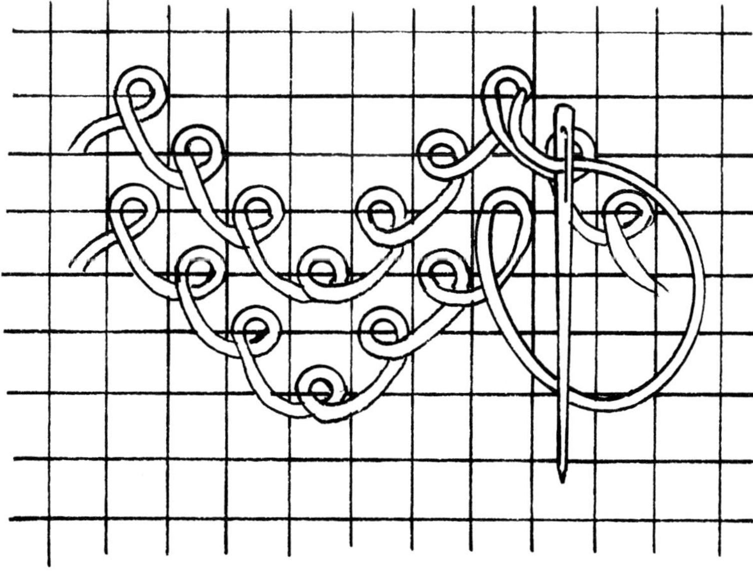

Fig. 37 Buttonhole chevrons

Fig. 38

Figs. 38, 39, 40, 41 The following four designs of the Four Seasons Tablecloth incorporate tambour work, Venetian embroidery, needlelace stitches, which include a number of different bars, picots and wheels. In that way most of the techniques in this book are pulled together. Joan Merrifield is working the tamboured areas which include the stitches given in this chapter. Liz Landry and the author have added their contribution. This is an ongoing project being worked for the Guild of Needlelaces by any of its members who have the time and the inclination to help

Fig. 39

autumn

Fig. 40

HERRINGBONE STITCH

This is a very useful stitch found in many laces that have a net foundation, it covers two meshes and three bars worked in the same way as in embroidery. The different shapes of the meshes change the character of the stitch. Worked on a diamond mesh, it becomes elongated, if worked on a hexagon mesh it appears squashed and flattened.

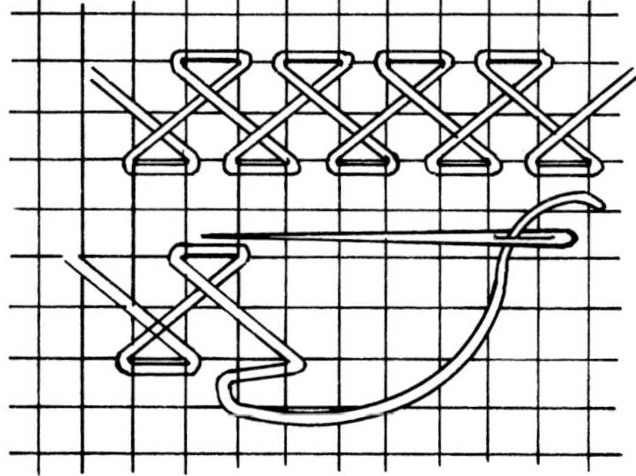

Fig. 42 Herringbone stitch

Fig. 41

Close Herringbone

This is also the stitch used to outline the leaves and petals. It is worked on the wrong side of the material to give a raised effect on the right side. When worked on fine linen lawn or muslin it becomes partly visible between two rows of back-stitching on the right side.

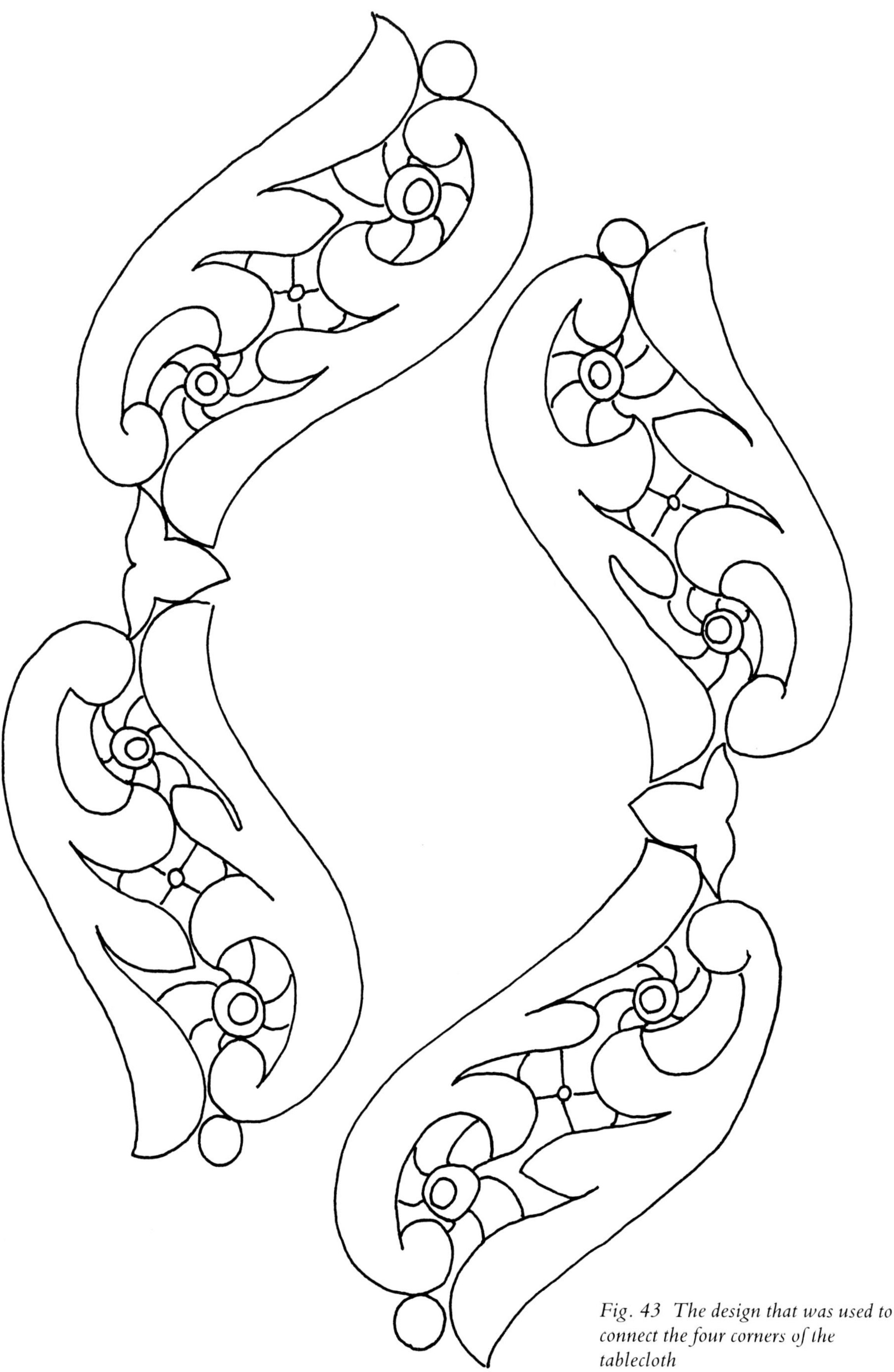

Fig. 43 The design that was used to connect the four corners of the tablecloth

◁*Photo 15 Four Seasons Tablecloth*

Fig. 44 Slanting or horizontal crossed stitch. For this stitch the diagram is probably easier to follow than the written word. It consists of a figure of eight stitch worked horizontally across a diamond mesh. Work through A and B, the needle is brought out at the bottom of the central diamond of the mesh and taken straight up across the middle of the figure of eight and in at the top point. It is brought out again under the left-hand point of the next diamond ready to work the next figure of eight

KNOTTED OR SLANTED CROSS STITCH

This is another filling stitch found in tambour and other needlerun laces. It is formed by working a figure of eight, worked horizontally, see *A* and *B*. The needle is brought out at the bottom point of the diamond and taken straight up across the middle of the figure of eight and back in at the top point. It should be taken out again under the left-hand point of the next diamond of the net ready to work the next figure of eight stitch.

Fig. 45 A design which was used on a scarf end and has been worked in Tambour work with inserts of needlepoint lace

Photo 16 A piece of Tambour lace presented to Joan Merrifield and worked by the Ladies of Lier, near Antwerp, Belgium

BIJ EEN ROOS
UIT LIERSE KANT

Hoe menig roos uit Lierse kant
ontbloeide in het Neteland!
Hoe menig «Zusterke-Begijn»
kon dáárom reeds gelukkig zijn!

Want tussen duim en tullen raam,
de vingers bruin-verweerd tezaam
ontsproot, gesponnen «hand bij hand»
een ranke roos uit witte kant...

Zo bloeit te Lier nog menig roos
als wonderbloem die, ver van broos,
ontbloeide uit het vinnig haken,
van die er kanten bloemen maken.

En met een hart uit Lierse kant
getuigt zij in het Neteland
dat elke bloem niet steeds verwelkt
maar soms voor eeuwen ... openkelkt!

Luc van Lierde

CONTINUOUS OR DETACHED RINGS

Take three threads of the material in both directions as the centre of each ring. Work three times round these threads darning under and over the threads of the warp and weft alternately.

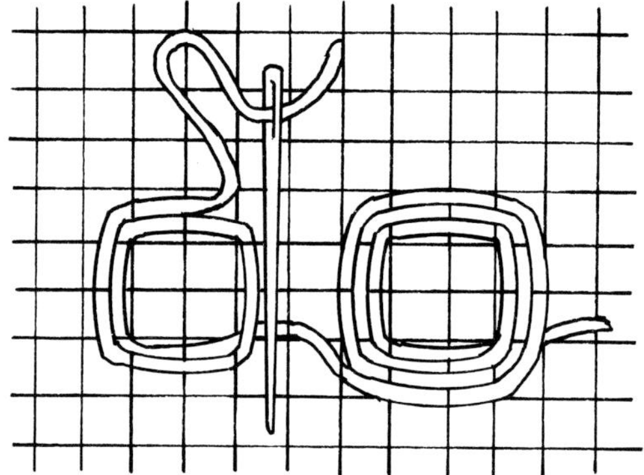

Fig. 46 Continuous or detached rings. These are worked by taking three threads of the material in both directions as the centre of each ring. Work three times round these threads darning under and over the thread of the warp and weft alternately

KNOTTED CHAIN OR SNAIL'S TRAIL

Insert the needle slantwise from left to right under two bars and a mesh. Pass the thread under the point of the needle from left to right and draw the thread up into a knot. Repeat to the bottom of the space being filled. Each row is cut and restarted at the top of the filling to keep the loops lying in the same direction. Two rows, one worked from top to bottom, then a second row worked by turning the work upside down and working down to the bottom gives a different appearance and a wider filling.

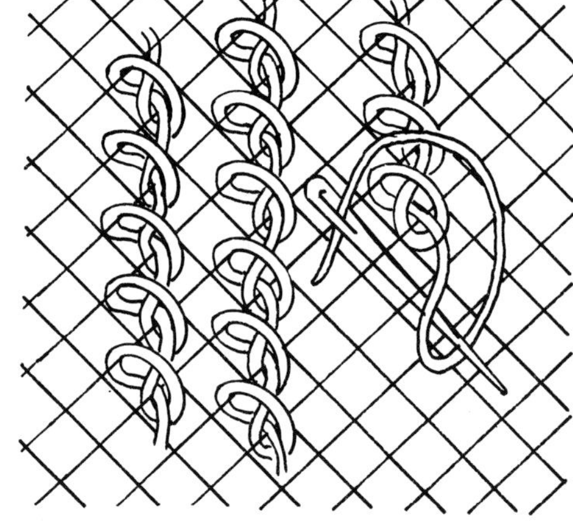

Fig. 47 Knotted chain is best worked in groups. Insert the needle at an angle, working from left to right, under two bars and a mesh (right to left if left-handed). Pass the thread under the point of the needle and draw the thread up into a knot

FIGURE OF EIGHT STITCH

The figure of eight is worked first in two continuous rows, see Fig. 1. Then the second set of stitches, which are shaded, is worked over both rows (Fig. 2).

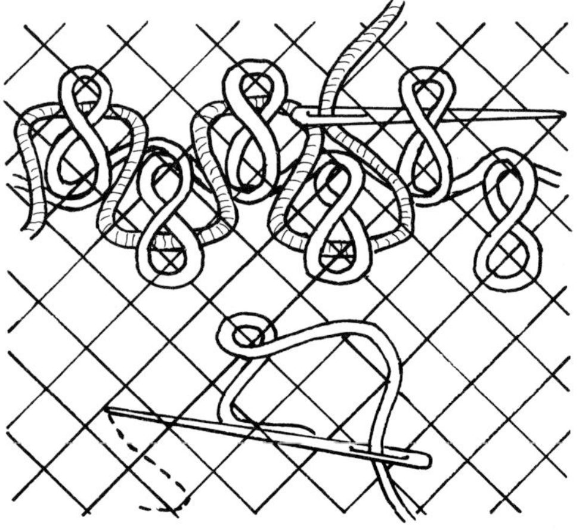

Fig. 48 Figure of eight and wave stitch consist of a figure of eight worked vertically in a zig-zag line on a diamond mesh and is interlaced with a second row of stitches

Fig. 49 A design by Jani Dubrick for a Hahlah cloth

Photo 17 White work that has tried to emulate Point de Gaz lace. It was common practice a generation ago, to mix pieces of lace together in this way. When large pieces of lace became worn, medallions of this sort were inserted to give the lace a new lease of life. Surface embroidery and pulled fabric stitches have been used on this particular piece to join small pieces of net together to form a flounce. Photograph by permission of May Arnfield

8 *Ayrshire embroidery*

This work was called sewed muslin to distinguish it from the Dresden pulled-work or the tambour embroidery. At the end of the Napoleonic Wars tamboured muslin gowns went out of fashion. The soft delicate effect of Dresden work was replaced by a different type of embroidery using a firmer quality muslin. Brighter colours became fashionable and the white muslin was used for ladies' indoor caps, for collars, cuffs and aprons, handkerchiefs, men's shirts and christening gowns. These gowns were passed down through the generations and can still be found in use today, in perfect condition, the treasured heirloom of the family. The style was reminiscent of the ladies' gowns of the late 1830–50s. It had a triangle for the front of the bodice, sometimes off the shoulder, the sleeves were either short puffed ones or layers of frills. There was a long embroidered panel, the full length of the skirt with a flat frill laid both sides of the panel which was called 'robbings'. The gowns were always of a floral design incorporating scrolls with the same flowing design as that of the bobbin lace of Caen or Chantilly and very often with the same spotted background. Most of the designing was done by professional draughtsmen based in Glasgow. The designs were very involved and beautiful and were stamped onto the muslin with a soluble water dye.

The stitches used were padded satin stitch, eyelets and cut-work. It is the delicate needlelace fillings in the cut-work that is the characteristic hallmark of this beautiful work. All the embroidery is worked first then the fine lace fillings are put in afterwards. If it is any consolation to our present day lacemakers, the work did not end up pristeen white but was collected from the out-workers and taken back to the depots to be washed, bleached, made up and boxed before being offered for sale. At one point it was possible to buy the muslin already stamped for the embroideress to work, it was even offered for sale in kit form, with the bodice, front panel and sleeves already embroidered. This left only the making up to be done, which could be undertaken by anyone capable of 'running up' a little dress. There was one snag to this short cut in that the cut-work and scallops also had to be cut and it was very easy to snip the embroidery or the lace fillings; the average dressmaker was not of the calibre of the original embroideresses. Too often the repair was carried out with a different size thread which did not help the overall effect.

Usually a christening robe came complete with a bonnet which had a circular lace medallion in the crown. It was made up of three sections, the crown, a back panel and the front piece. Another common design was an egg-shaped back panel and an oblong strip that went over the baby's head. The bonnets were made in such a way that they could be drawn up to fit a new baby, then gradually the draw strings could be released to enlarge the bonnet as the child grew older. The diagram and the photographs accompanying this chapter illustrate this quite clearly.

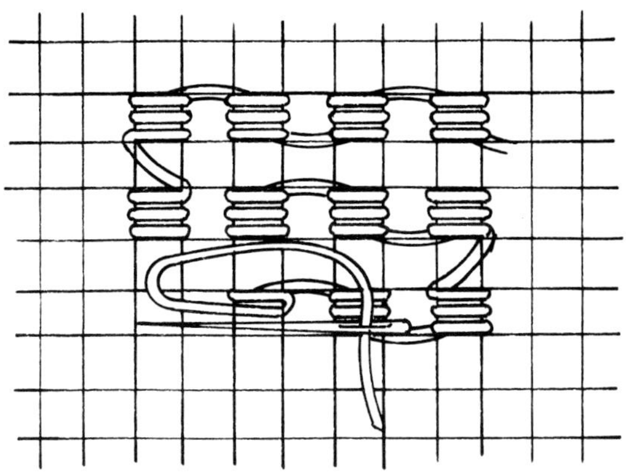

Fig. 50 Satin stitch dots. The number of stitches used to form a dot and the number of threads of material it is worked over will depend on the weight of the linen

Photo 18 This antique doll's clothes were made and embroidered by the author, combining Ayrshire embroidery with Bobbin lace. The doll is 13in high

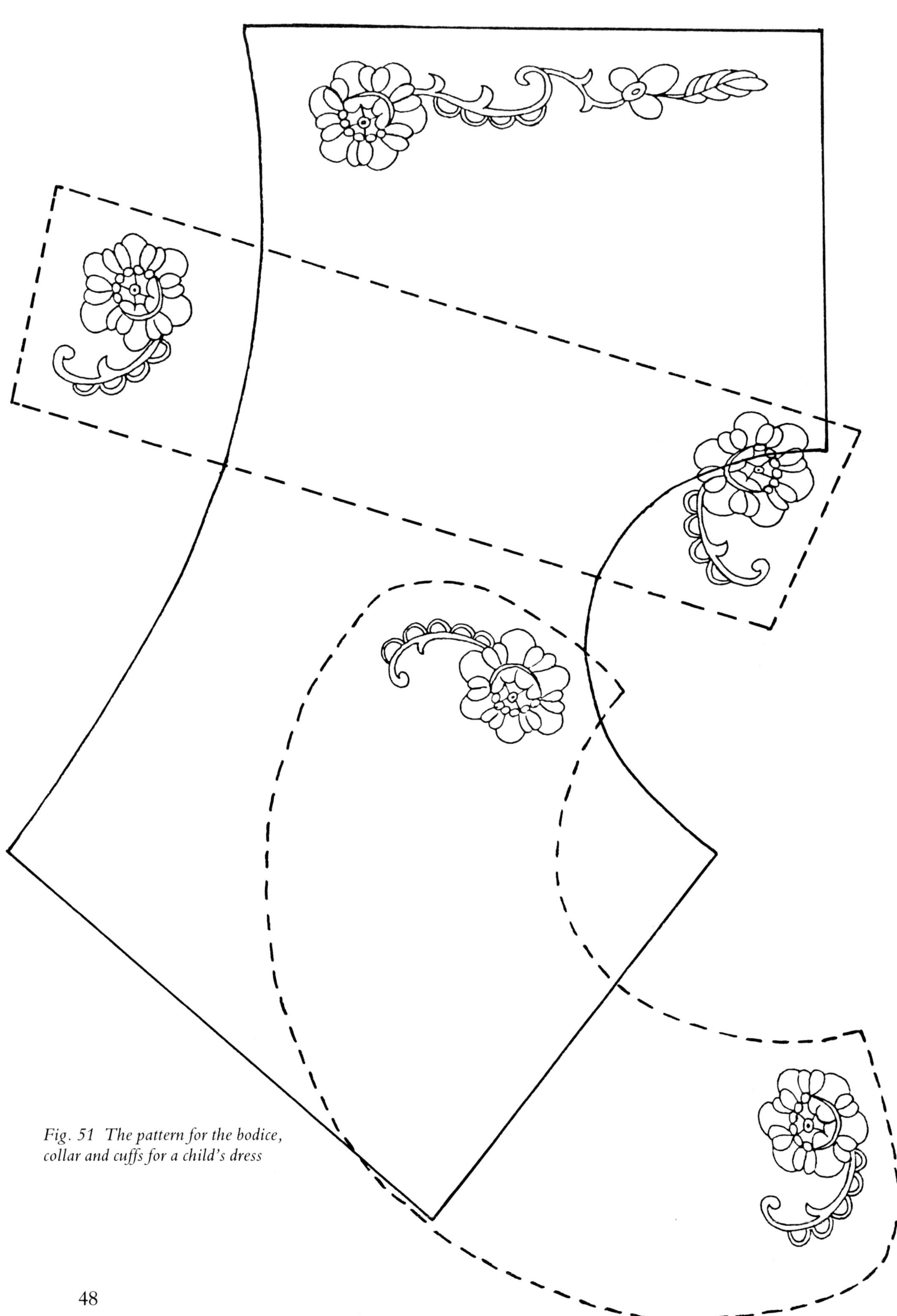

Fig. 51 The pattern for the bodice, collar and cuffs for a child's dress

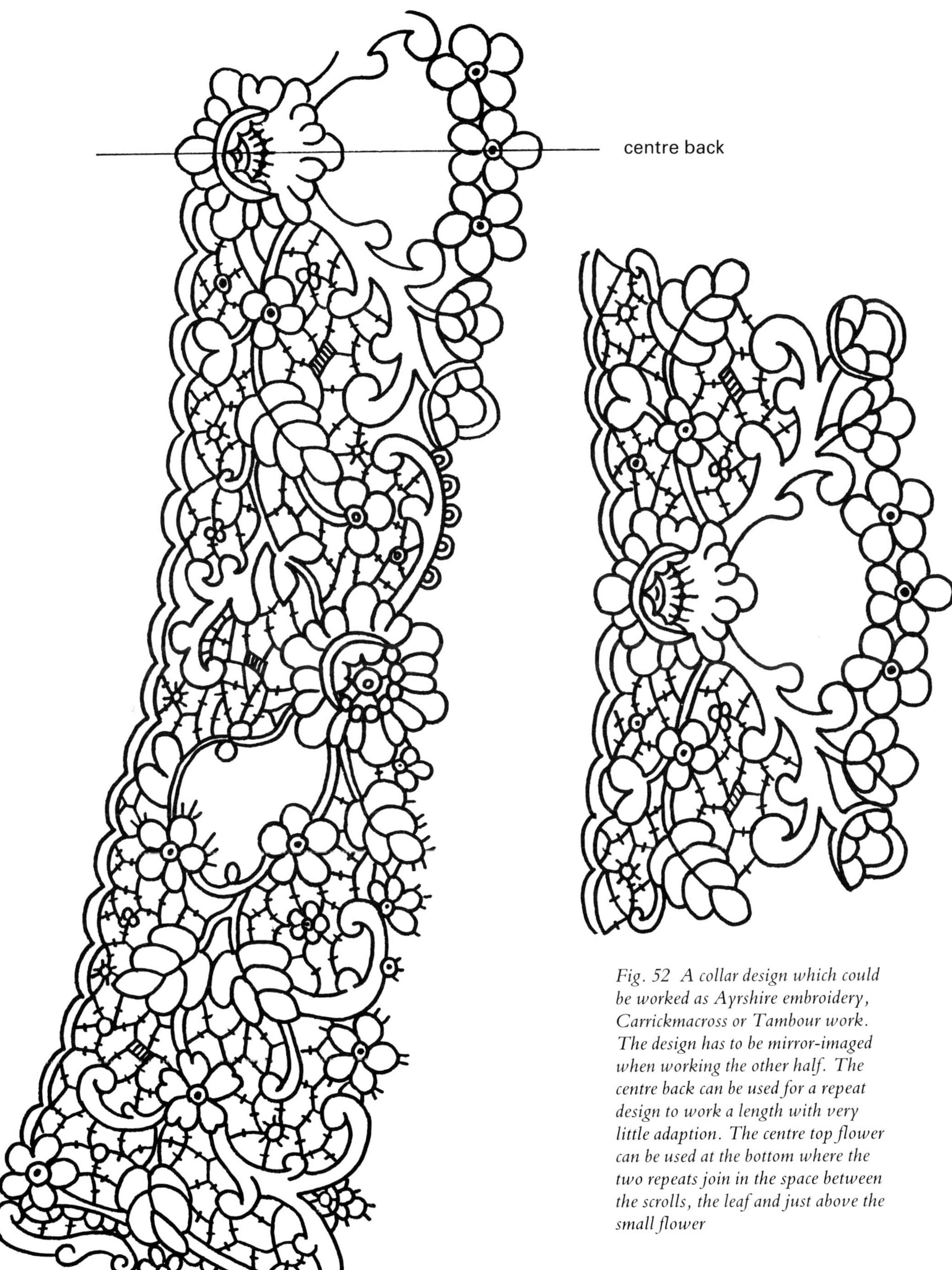

Fig. 52 A collar design which could be worked as Ayrshire embroidery, Carrickmacross or Tambour work. The design has to be mirror-imaged when working the other half. The centre back can be used for a repeat design to work a length with very little adaption. The centre top flower can be used at the bottom where the two repeats join in the space between the scrolls, the leaf and just above the small flower

Photo 19 A bonnet in Ayrshire embroidery. A smocking transfer was used for the spacing of the padded dots. The design of the embroidery was used again for the sleeve of the doll's dress and was worked by the author

Photo 20 The bells in this piece of work have been formed by the application of embroidered petals. Property of May Arnfield

Photo 21 This small snippet of Dresden lace has been enlarged to four times its actual size to allow the minute stitchery to be seen. The linen lawn that has been used is exceedingly fine, as is the thread which at a rough estimate is about 300/s

9 Venetian embroidery

Photo 22 A piece of Venetian embroidery worked by Liz Landry. Diagrams for the stitches used are given on page 53, Fig. 54

This is a compact embroidery that combines counted thread with cut-work and an added raised cordonnette gives the effect of early Venetian Gros Point. It works well with quilting so would be an ideal technique for jackets or waistcoats etc and apart from dress it is useful for household items.

A fine linen material is the best choice, but do take into consideration the fact that the surface stitchery is worked over the counted threads. Therefore the weight of the material will depend on the individual's eyesight. After transferring the design onto the material it is best mounted in a frame to work the surface stitches for the fillings. These can be counted thread or canvas work stitches apart from the ones used in the sample. Those worked on the sample are from an original piece of Venetian embroidery. The size of the thread used for the surface stitches is the same thickness as the threads of the material being worked on. When this part of the work is finished it is taken out of the frame and mounted onto a backing material.

The bars are worked next, in all old samples only one type of bar is used, that of the three laid threads buttonholed over, without any picots. When laying in the bars catch each end well over the edge of the design so that the ends of the bars lay under the cordonnette, adding strength to the embroidery.

There are two schools of thought on how the cordonnette should be worked. One is that the material is cut away before the cordonnette is worked, the other is that all stitchery is worked before the material is cut. Maybe when the first book was written the material was not so likely to fray, whereas the author of the Weldon book written at the turn of the century found it too much of a hassle coping with machine woven material and decided it was best to cut last. It can work both ways as long as the first way has a substantial cordonnette to work over and the material is well mounted on the backing.

When using Venetian embroidery in conjunction with quilting the embroidery is finished and removed from the backing material. The surplus material cut away from behind the bars and round the cordonnette outline. Lay the motif on the material to be quilted which should be of a different toning colour, and trace the outline. This is best done with tacking stitches although a soluble ink, felt-tip embroidery pencil can be used. Lift away the motif and work the quilting right to the edge of the tracing. Any quilting technique can be used and again the Elna TX has been used for backing of the sampler.

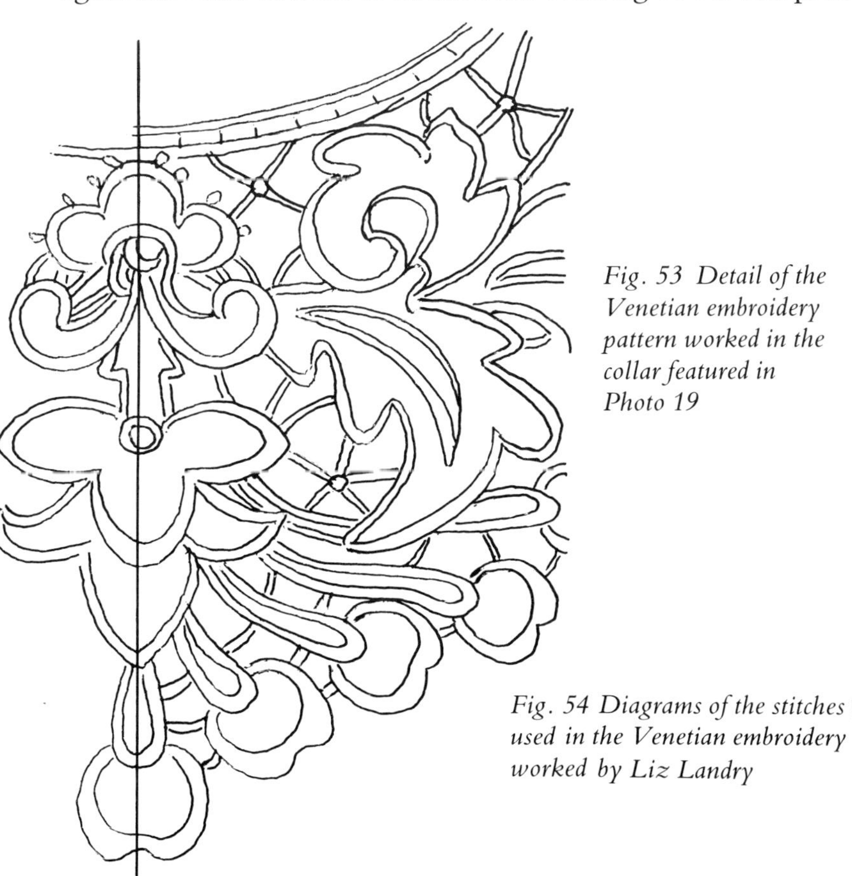

Fig. 53 Detail of the Venetian embroidery pattern worked in the collar featured in Photo 19

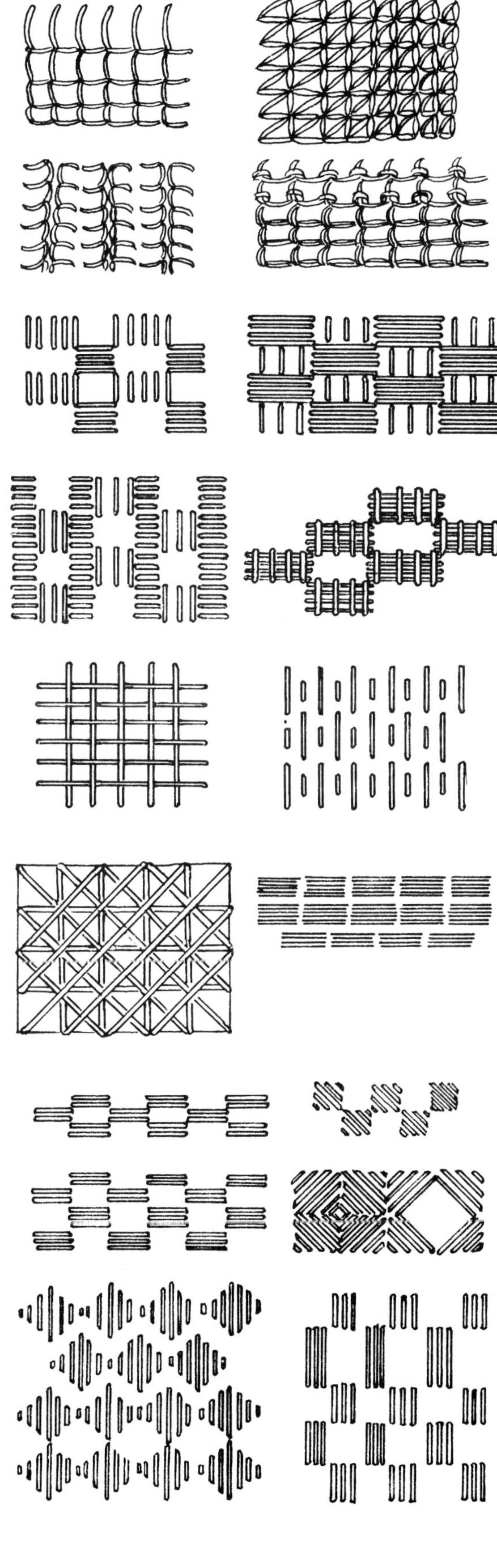

Fig. 54 Diagrams of the stitches used in the Venetian embroidery worked by Liz Landry ▷

1

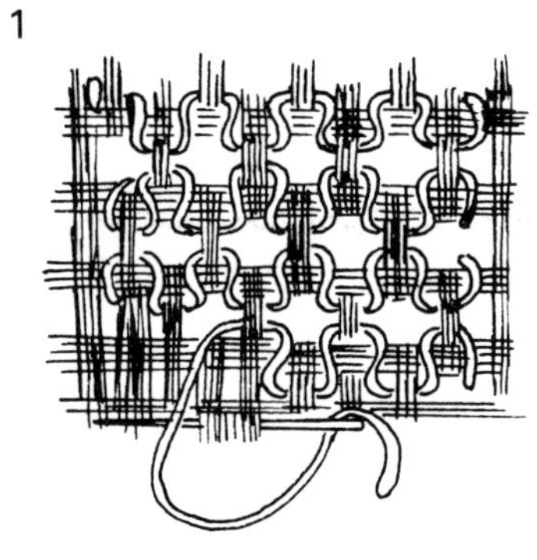

5

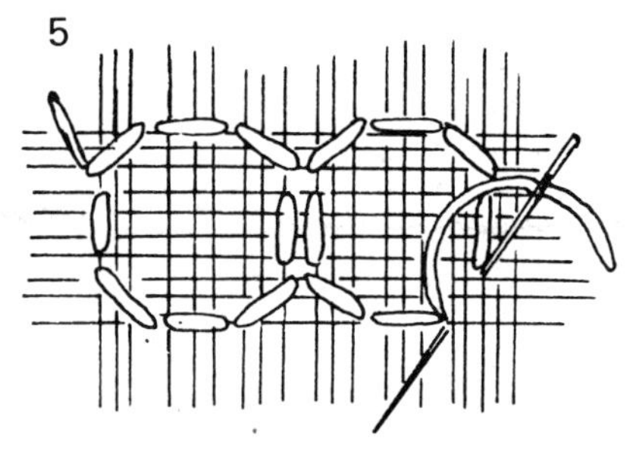

2

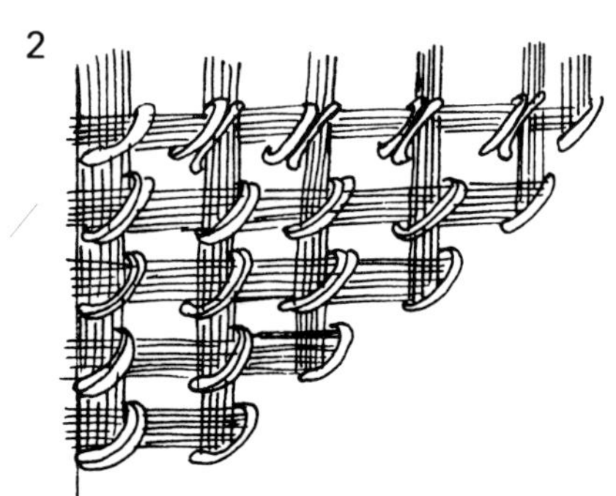

6

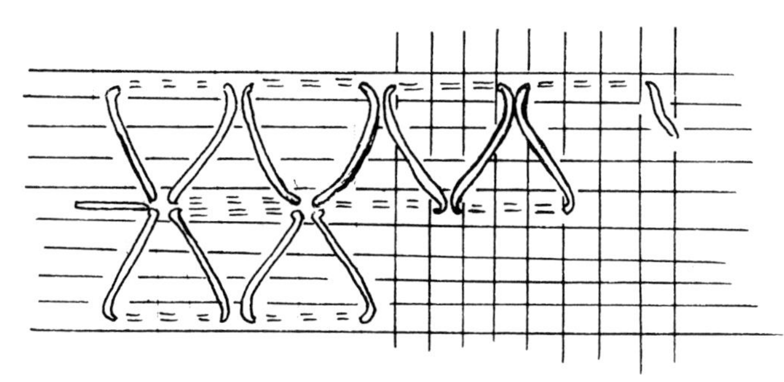

3

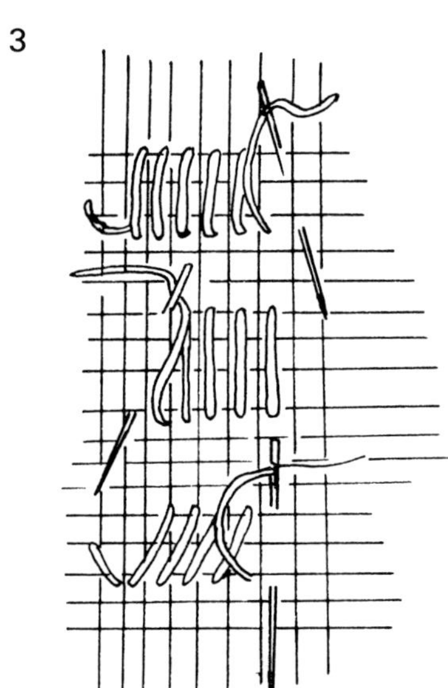

7

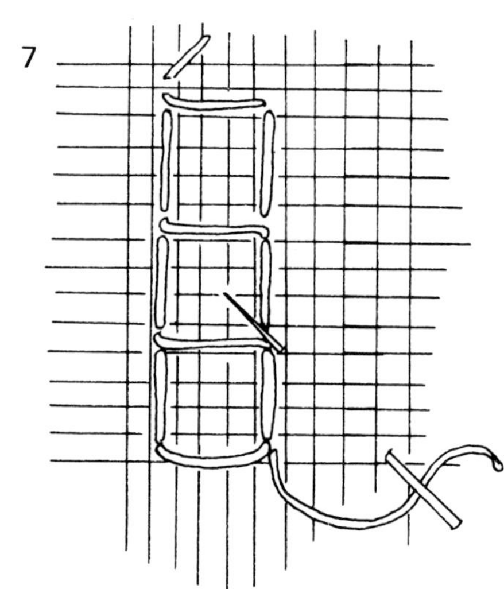

4

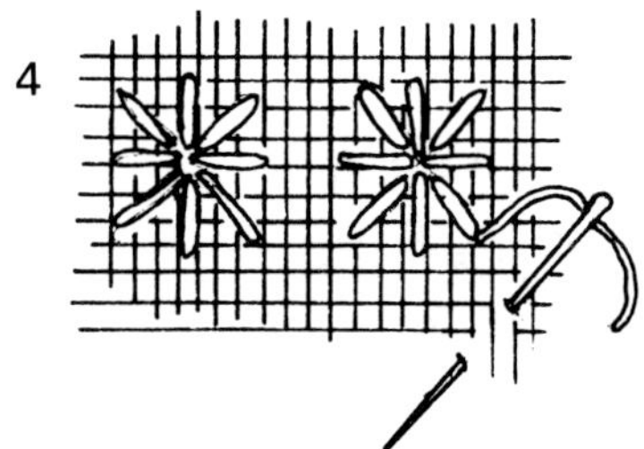

Fig. 55 These stitches are all drawn fabric techniques used in working the little bird shown in the photograph on page 55. All these stitches can be used as surface stitches for Venetian embroidery if allowed to lie on the surface without the tight tension being used.

1. Wave stitch, the working thread must be pulled tight and an even tension will give uniform holes.

2. Faggot stitch on the diagonal.

3. Fillings based on Satin stitch.

4. A Star eyelet which consists of eight stitches worked from a central point.

5. Ringed back stitch.

6. Window filling, is wave stitch worked over an uneven number of threads.

7. Square filling, sometimes known as Cobbler filling, is easily worked by following the diagram.

These stitches are the main ones used in the pieces by Vera Nichols

◁ *Photo 23 This design shows pulled fabric techniques combined with surface stitches and raised cordonnette outline. Worked by Vera Nichols*

Photo 24 An example of pulled fabric stitches combined with raised areas of knots and buttonhole rings. The whole design has the added concept of a raised cordonnet. Worked by Vera Nichols

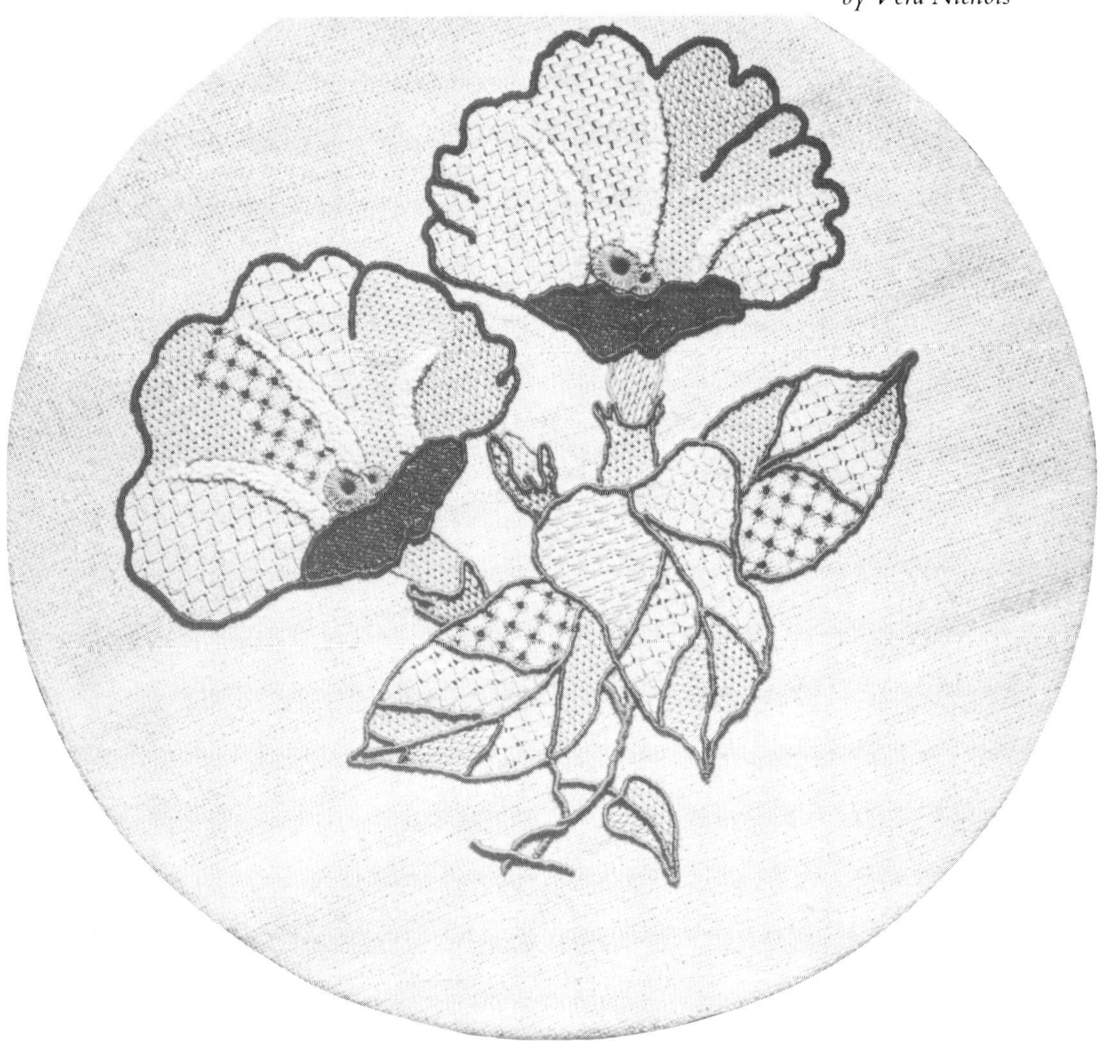

Fig. 56 A conventional cut-work design which is being worked as Venetian embroidery along the edge of a circular tablecloth. The same design will be used for a lampshade to match

◁ *Photo 25 At first glance this embroidery can be confused with Bobbin lace. It is pulled fabric work based on a Torchon lace pattern from* Knypperskan Vol. III, *and is worked with a thick and fine thread on scrim material*

Photo 26 Drawn thread work combined with surface stitchery using the hardanger technique. This piece was worked by the author

BOX 1

Work in height and width over six threads, to ensure the right count has been made, work a running stitch over six and under six threads the width and the length of the square.

Working down the side of the square, cut six threads on one side and withdraw them across to the running stitches on the opposite side. Leave six threads then cut and withdraw the next six threads in the same way.

Continue down to the bottom of the square.

Working along the top of the square, cut six threads and leave six threads and withdraw the cut threads to the bottom of the square.

The drawn threads can be whipped along the outline of the shape to be used as part of the padding for the cordonnette, or cut off at the appropriate place and the outline of the square or shape can be buttonholed round after the fillings are worked.

Execute the filling by working vertically down the lines, making a buttonhole stitch over three threads to the left, over three threads in the top, over three to the right and over three into the bottom of the square.

Take the needle up and over the first buttonhole stitch on the left and weave down behind the six threads to work the next square.

The working thread is hidden behind the blocks or squares of material and oval holes are formed between each square.

Fig. 57

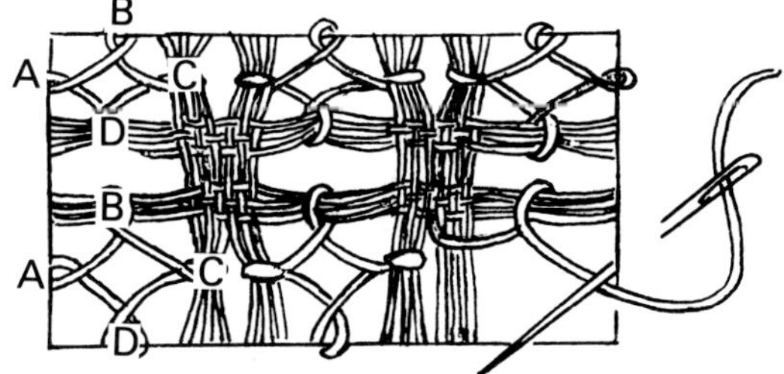

Fig. 58 The centre from one part of the design given in the tambour section, which could be utilised for drawn thread, bar or ladder work and surface embroidery

BOX 2

For this pattern the stitches are worked in diagonal lines.

The working thread is again passed behind the square left in the material. Start in the top left-hand corner.

Work the left-hand side of the block, then to the top, to the right, then the bottom.

Weave along to the next square on the diagonal line and work the buttonhole stitches in the same order, left, top, right and bottom.

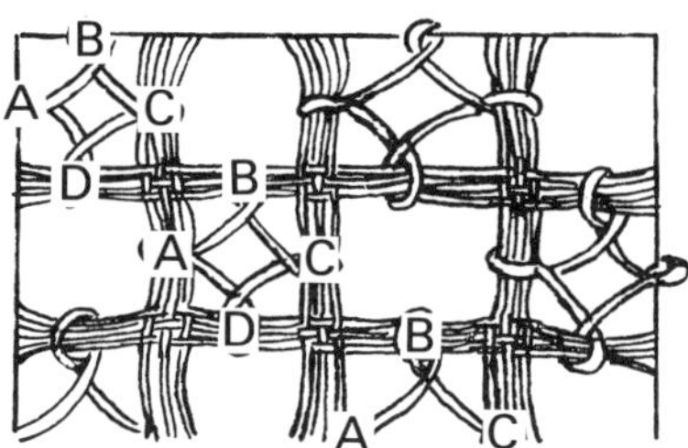

Fig. 59

BOX 3

Ladder Hem stitch is worked both top and bottom of a row of drawn threads.

Draw out the number of threads according to the width needed.

Fasten the thread on the left and slip the needle in from right to left under three or four warp threads.

Draw out and insert upwards under two threads of the weft.

Finish along the top row then turn the work round and make the second row of stitches in the same way.

Fig. 60

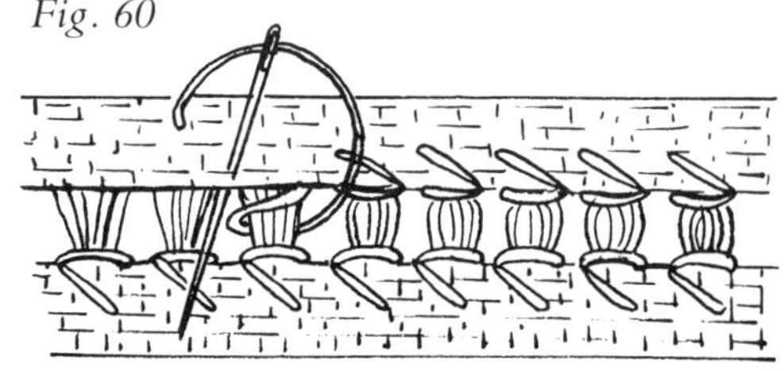

Fig. 61

BOX 4

Rows of darning stitches worked under and over clusters of three threads, worked on the diagonal. Follow the sequence shown in the drawing.

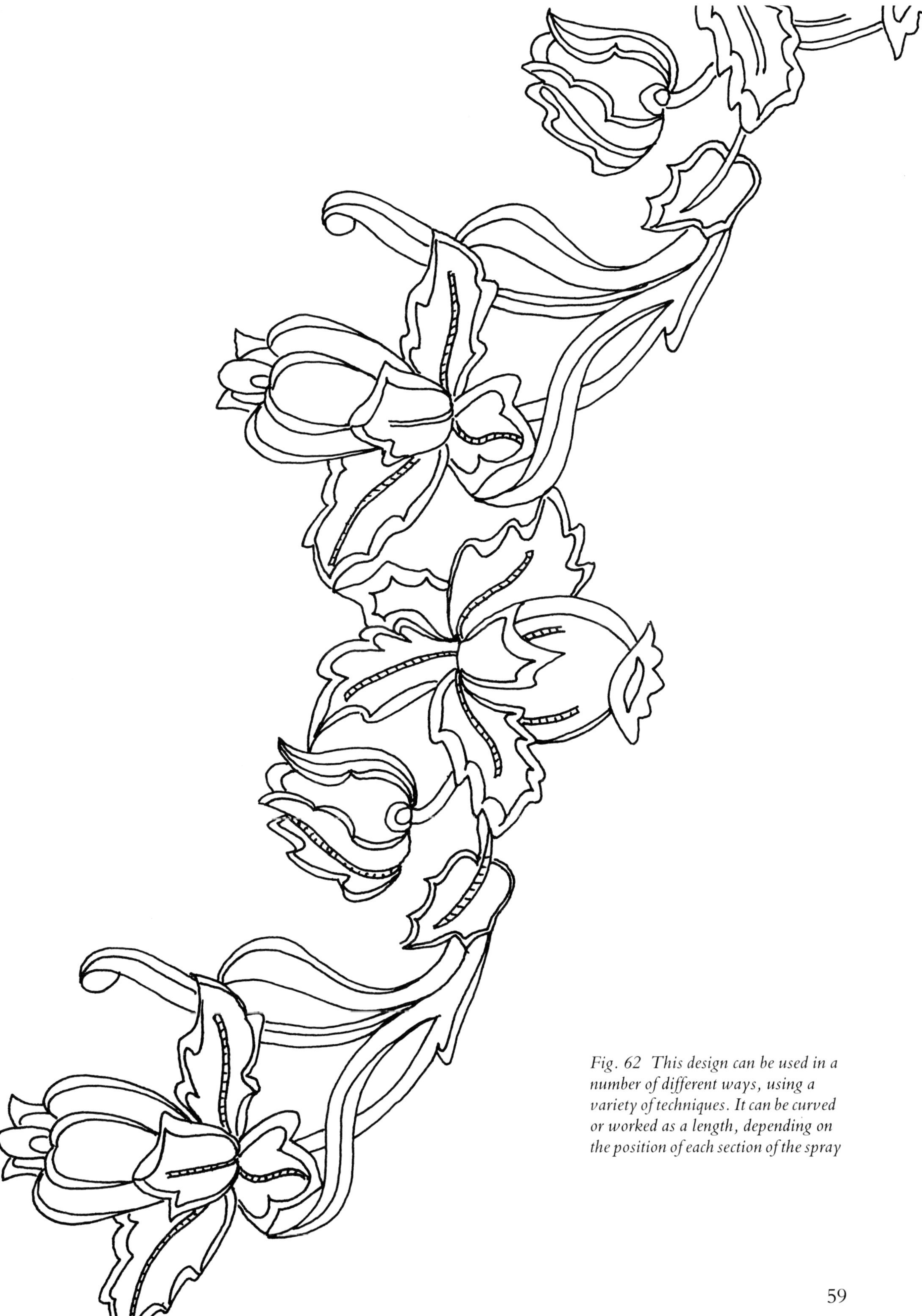

Fig. 62 This design can be used in a number of different ways, using a variety of techniques. It can be curved or worked as a length, depending on the position of each section of the spray

It is possible to curve a straight-edge design into a collar.

Cut a collar shape to suit out of calico. Redraw the actual design, discarding all bars. The solid motifs along the bottom line of the design given are now placed so that each scroll, leaf and flower lays side by side along the inside curve of the collar (Fig. 2).

The direction of the lay of the leaves and scrolls along the top will be altered. To allow for adjusting the curve, cut between the end scroll of one leaf and the stalk of the second leaf where marked on the design.

Redraw the line of scallops and half wheels along the top of the design. It will be necessary to cut between each side of the centre scallop to make the line curve and extra sections will be needed to cover the outer line of the design because of it being opened up.

Stick the paper design into place on the calico, working from the inside curve of the collar to the outside edge. Then stitch the design of scallops and half wheels round the outside edge.

Draw in all the bars, pencil them directly onto the calico. A wheel can be incorporated between the leaves and flowers to act as an infill if needed.

A sheet of clear acetate film can be stuck over the pattern to keep it permanent or the design can be drawn in by tracing round the paper directly onto the calico.

This design has been chosen as an exercise because it can be adapted to be worked in any of the techniques covered in this book or can be used as a needlepoint lace design.

Fig. 63 An exercise in the use of bars

10 Spanish embroidered lace

This is a lace that is made in imitation of the hand-made raised Spanish Points. It is worked on fine linen, using a cordonnette to raise the design and a fine linen thread.

Transfer the design onto a plain, fine linen or muslin then back with material and draughtsman's line.

The ground is a réseau for Point de Venise or Pea stitch, making sure that at no time the linen beneath is picked up accidently by the needle. When the ground is finished, lay a cordonnette round all the outlines of the pattern and couch to the linen beneath. Buttonhole the cordonnette making sure each stitch takes up the linen material underneath. In early examples of this work the cordonnette is varied in width by the addition of extra threads in the same way as Venetian lace. The couch stitches are cut from behind to release the embroidery and the linen is cut from behind the réseau, leaving the design to stand bold of the background.

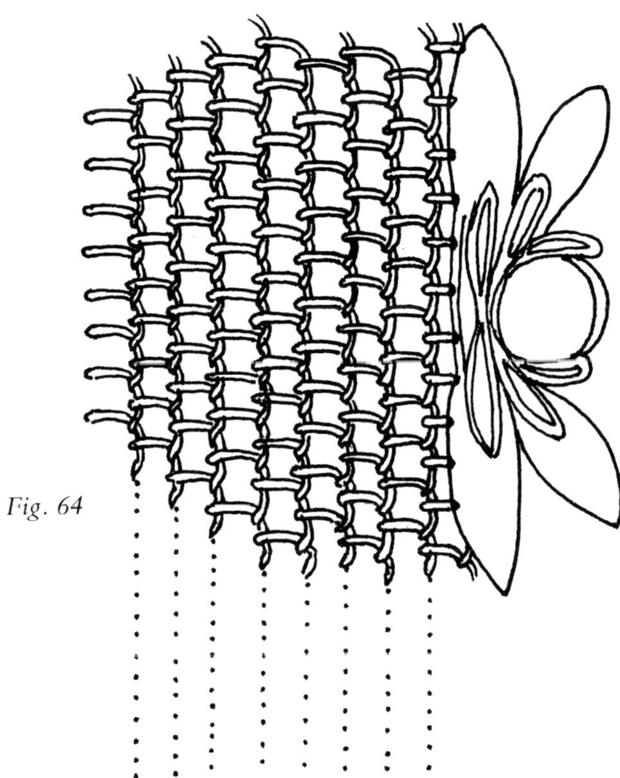

Fig. 64

Fig 65 This design can be adapted ▷ for any number of uses. In its original form three motifs were added to form a wedding head-dress, worked in oyster and shell-pink silk. The top outline was worked over a fine flower wire

11 *A new way with Carrickmacross*

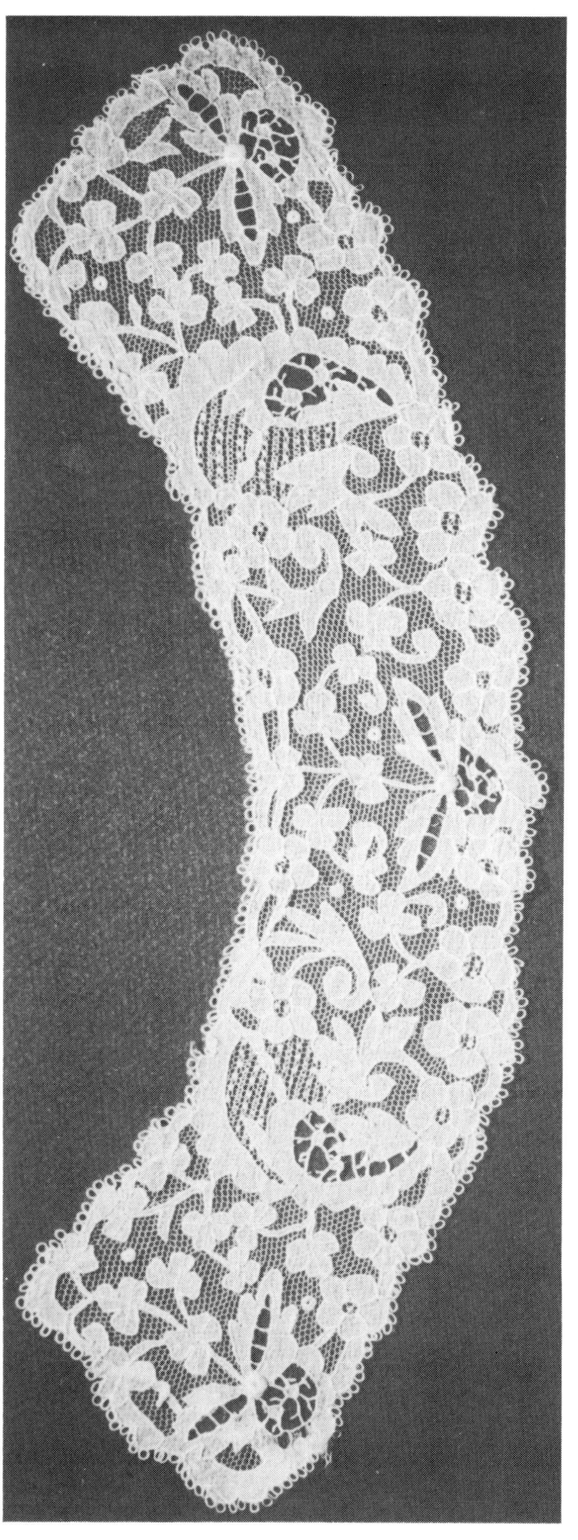

The box being worked by Shirley Warren shows the use of hand-dyed material to get the tints and shades to match the threads. The jacket was worked with threads to match the tints and shades of the flowers. Why? Because the petals are taken from silk flowers already dyed. The flowers were taken apart, each petal mounted onto backing material and the edges whipped over. Care has to be taken that the edges of the petals that are cut on the cross grain of the materials do not pull away. A cordonnette was laid and buttonholed closely round each petal then removed from the backing and placed in position on the jacket. The clouds were worked by using a fine knitting ribbon in the same way as a tape would be laid, being silk it gives a sheen against tape which would be too heavy for the rest of the work. The size of the petals will depend on what it is to be used for. The collar and continuous length can be worked from hydrangea heads. One spray has enough flowerlets to make up a collar. The flower petals would be worked individually, then laid to the pattern of the collar and joined with bars, Gütermann 100/35 was used for the jacket, a fine silk used for the collar and length. Packets of loose petals are available which can save time unpicking the flowers and at the same time cheaper.

Photo 27 One half of a Peter Pan collar worked in tamboured Carrickmacross lace on net. The edge is formed by twisting the cordonnet into a backward loop and catching each loop down with a zig-zag stitch

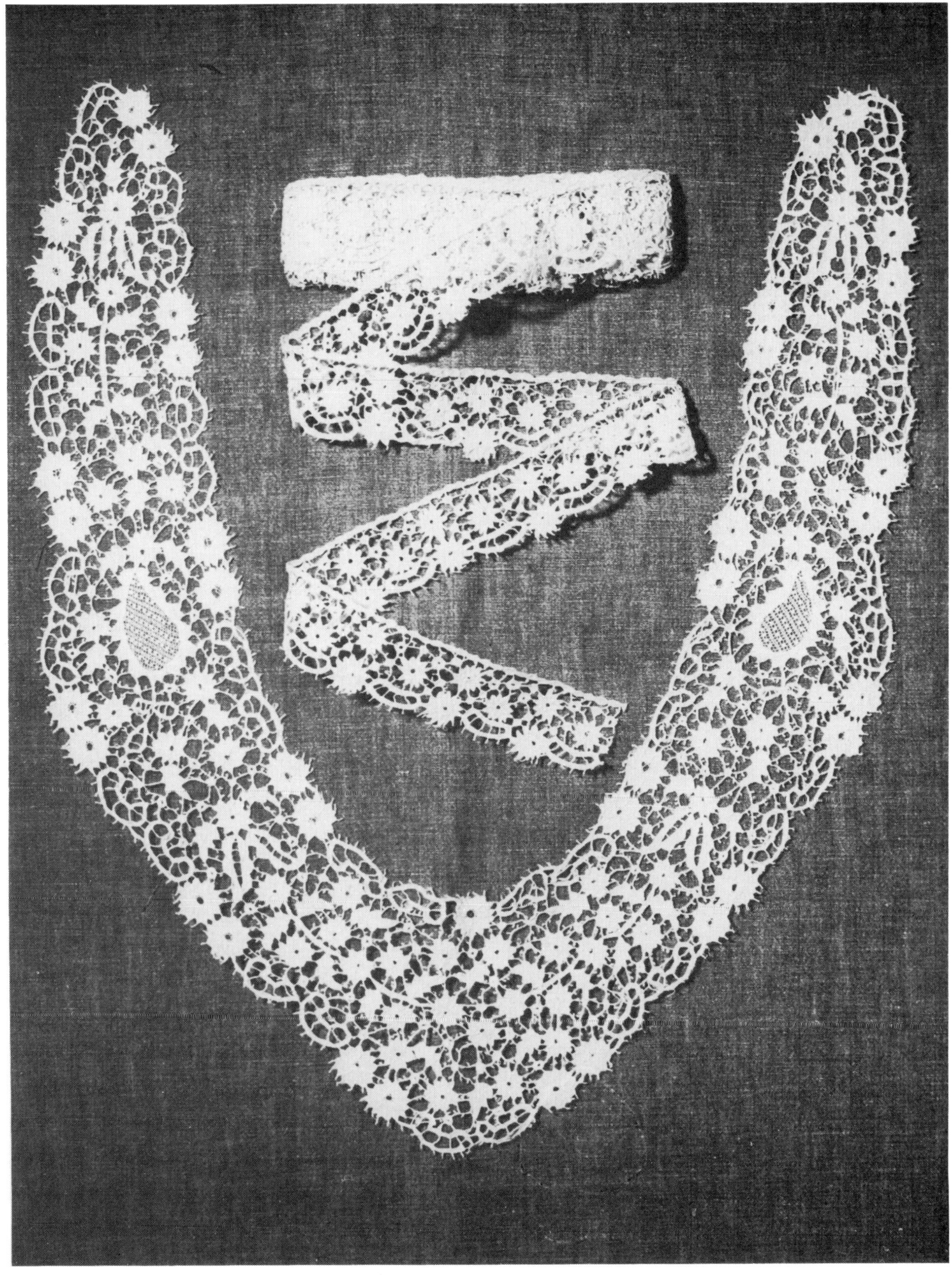

Photo 28

Photo 29 This shows the use of silk flowers and knitting ribbon applied to the front of a jacket

Fig. 66 The outline for the clouds shown in the photograph on page 64 which has needlepoint fillings

Lace can be inserted into a background of quilting (as shown in Photo 30) to give completely different textures. Carrickmacross can be enriched with surface stitchery as can be seen in the photograph of the cuff. Fabric printing can be used on any material before the embroidery is added. Ayrshire embroidery need not be white work and Richelieu looks good worked in silk on silk instead of the more usual white on

white. The net for tambour work can also be printed with fabric dyes. The dyed net could help fill in a design even quicker than the tambour fillings.

The butterfly is needlepoint lace worked from a laid cordonnet so the jacket combines the embroidery with lace.

The clown picture is using needlepoint lace in an unconventional way so why can't all the techniques in the book be intermingled?

Photo 30 The back of a baby's bonnet. Raised dots, pulled fabric stitches and quilting have all been combined in this piece of work which is seventeenth century and belongs to Catherine Barley

Fig. 67

Photo 31 To the needlepoint lace of today. This design has been worked by Nina Devereux as a finale for this book

Further reading

d'Arcy, Eithne, *Irish Crochet Lace*, Dryad Press
Channer, C C, *Lacemaking Point Ground*, Dryad Press
Earnshaw, Pat, *Lace in Fashion*, Batsford
Fisher, Jennifer, *Tape and Braid Lace for Today*, Dryad Press
Fisher, Jennifer, *Torchon Lace for Today*, Dryad Press
Houston-Almqvist, Jane, *Mountmellick Work: Irish White Embroidery* , Dryad Press
Konior, Mary, *Pattern Book of Tatting*, Dryad Press
Lovesey, Nenia, *Introduction to Needlepoint Lace*, Batsford
Lovesey, Nenia, *Creative Design in Needlepoint Lace*, Batsford
Lovesey, Nenia, *Technique of Needlepoint Lace*, Batsford
Lovesey, Nenia, and Barley, Catherine, *Venetian Gros Point Lace*, Dryad Press
O'Cleirigh, Nellie, *Carrickmacross Lace*, Dryad Press
O'Connor, Eileen, *Irish Lacemaking*, Dryad Press
Sorenson, Veronica, *Modern Lace Design*, Batsford

Suppliers

A. Sells
'Lane Cove'
49 PedleyLane
Clifton
Shefford
Beds
Equipment, threads and books

Mace and Nairn
89 Crane Street
Salisbury
Wilts
Threads and equipment

Sebalace
76 Main Street
Addingham
Ilkley
West Yorks
All lacemaking requisites

John & Jennifer Ford
5 Squirrels Hollow
Boney Way
Walsall
All lacemaking requisites and bobbin-maker

Shireburn Lace
Finkle Court
Finkle
Sherburn in Elmet
North Yorks
Lace specialist

Teazle Embroideries
35 Boothferry Road
Hull
North Humberside
Needlepoint lace specialist

The Editor
Guild of Needlelaces
39 Napier Road
Crowthorne
Berkshire

The Lace Guild
c/o The Hollies
53 Audnam
Stourbridge
West Midlands

Deka Fabric Paints
Blythe Road
Hammersmith
London W14

Transfers
Deighton Bros Ltd
Riverside Road
Barnstaple
North Devon

Silks & Silk
Jack Piper
Silverdale
Flax Lane
Glemsford
Suffolk

The English Lace School
Honiton Court
Rockbeare
Nr. Exeter
Devon
Books, threads, needles, pins, etc.

G. Hall
90 Shrewsbury Crescent
Humbledon
Tyne and Wear
Afficots, ring boxes and other fine tools

Newham Lace Equipment
15 Marlow Close
Basingstoke
Hants

Index